Günter von Hummel

Visions: The 'other way round'
of Love and Death

Theory and Practice of a new Method
for Self-Experience and -Therapy

The cover picture by E. Nolde has the title high camber wave 1. Nolde's sea pictures are something that may be called 'visions'. They are not abstract, but also only implied figurative. With 'vision', indeed, a state of the earliest psychic constitutions of man can be described, in which no fixed psychic structure is yet present. Nevertheless, one must return to this state in order to regenerate from there and in order to be able to build up anew in the sense of a maturation and completion, to which more belongs. Namely 'one more', which also represents a word play to the high camber wave 1 of which the speech will still be.

Production and Publishing
BoD - Books on Demand, Norderstedt, Germany
ISBN 9783754395820

Table of Contents

1. The ‚other way round' of Love
   and Death 5
2. Lacan's Triple Braid 30
3. Making a Feast 48
4. 'Iconic' and Female Discourse of Love ... 66
5. Death, the absolute Master? 92
6. 'Leave him out' 110
7. Visions 'the other way round' 124
8. Lacan's 'Thing' and the Awareness of
   Mechthild of Magdeburg 148
   Adnexe 161
   Bibliography 173

1. The other way round of Love and Death

In the ZEIT of 27. 5. 2021 a young woman writes about the experiences and sufferings of her mental illness. "Taking mentally ill people seriously for once and presenting them authentically", is written in the preface of her text.[1] And indeed, she describes her illness, including hospitalization and everyday situations, very meticulously, but also in a differentiated way. Above all, she deals with the way in which mental symptomatology comes across as superficial, misleading and unhelpful in Netflix series and other cinematic and verbal representations. She describes how in the series '13 Reasons Why' the psychotherapist "says with a serious face and reassuring voice: Sometimes things get worse before they get better." Grandiose, typical pseudo-logic, which the author can only ever counter with the statement that the true superpower lies 'in enduring alone'.

But why does she say that she is mentally ill? Isn't this just an expression of the professionally established and the perfectly adapted, who follow the so-called 'university discourse', while the author herself argues in a much more empathetic, self-organized and fundamental way, so that one could call her a protagonist not only in her own cause? Is she not almost a psychoanalyst, one for herself

---

[1] Grellmann, L., Well, that's a bit too crazy for me, ZEIT No. 22 (2021) p. 68

and one for others concerned? She is neurotic, but the essence of neurosis is basically only that the neurotic not only imagines and loves his fantasies, but that he enjoys them intimately. He passionately enjoys what he fantasizes as floridly as if it were real. Neurosis is psychologically not okay, but is it also illness?

When St. Mechthild of Magdeburg (1207-1282) confessed to her head nurse: "God speaks to me"! the latter was not at all 'amused'. However, the nuns were designed to communicate with God. But suddenly one of them seems to dance out of the ranks and yet everyone gets confused. The colleagues are jealous, the superiors fear for the orthodoxy. "Those who love a lot are blissfully silent, those who do not love are the watchdogs [traitors] of love," she wrote herself.[2] For years I cared for Catholic sisters in a home for the elderly that belonged to them, as a doctor. They were all modest, content and well to do. But it never occurred to them that God might one day directly alleviate their suffering. Why, actually? I would say, because today's time has become even more than before the watchdogs of love and therefore they did not know anything about this 'other way round' of the 'Flowing Light' (Mechthild's main work), of which I want to report here later from a modern point of view.

It is well known that most psychoanalysts, starting with

---

[2] Mechthild von Magdeburg, The Flowing Light of the Godhead, Publishing House of World Religions (2010) VI, 25

Freud, consider themselves atheists. But the French psychoanalyst J. Lacan scoffed at this and said that one could see well "that God intervenes daily in people's lives, for example in the form of a woman. The preachers and the women are the worst troublemakers," he stated. Well, one may not have to see it so blatantly, but the idea that it can be the most diverse things, the causation of which one does not know, allows for all sorts of speculations. Perhaps St. Mechthild took the causation as divine too seriously, too exaggerated, too maniform.

But in her case it is not a matter of fantasies, but of 'visions', which I write in quotation marks for the time being because of certain ambiguities. Having fantasies is not the problem either, but letting oneself be too strongly excited by them - often unconsciously - is not. The subtle artists, teachers, masters and 'visionaries' of mankind could always be accused of being a bit 'mentally ill', they just didn't do as much self-incrimination as the author above. To enjoy always belongs some insanity anyway and even the philosopher F. W. Hegel once said that he personally would have been close to mental illness for a short time, so much he enjoyed his thoughts. Among such neurotics one can also count the poet A. Strindberg, the composer R. Schuhmann, the painter E. Munch and many others from culture and science. But in the meantime things have changed, we have psychoanalysis!?

It is not unknown that philosophers are often hostile to psychoanalysis. One cannot blame such a populist thinker as D. Precht, he has simply not informed himself enough about what Sigmund Freud or the French psychoanalyst Jacques Lacan have said and written. But with the currently greatest philosopher in Central Europe, Jürgen Habermas, this is more than surprising. If laymen feel repelled by Freud's sexual theory, one can still understand that. They believe that it is about sexuality - in the first place at least - but this is only a side effect, the word 'sexual' only denotes a characteristic of the basic forces of human desire, which are already formed in earliest childhood and have just the character of drives, which inevitably, as if penetratingly, head for their goal in order to pacify themselves.

Habermas, however, thinks that Freud, and Lacan in particular, "darkened the light of the Enlightenment" with his psychoanalytic theory. But this negative statement must be reinterpreted positively: the light of the Enlightenment was not as bright as Habermas thinks; the nineteenth and twentieth centuries, with their horrific wars, have shown that the most terrible darkness prevailed, which the Enlightenment did nothing to change. And so it could only be good to dim the light of the Enlightenment a bit with an excursion into psychoanalysis. Freud's fundamental forces concern the eros-life and death drives, that is - if I may put it very simplistically and sweepingly - the power of love and death. But precisely because this is only expressed in a very simplistic way, I have written in the title of the book of the 'other way round' of these forces and also of psychoanalysis as a whole. Because 'visions' have no validity in it.

That they are not completely disregarded is mainly due to the French psychoanalyst J. Lacan, who reformulated these two forces into the power of a perceptual or viewing drive (close to love) and an expressive or speech drive (close to death). In any case, with this reformulation psychoanalysis can be better understood and more comprehensively used. It is not incomprehensible that speaking is close to death. People constantly talk past each other, they misunderstand each other, even they lie, they often contradict each other in a total, perfect way, so that one really has to ask oneself what they actually have from speaking, from communicating.

Not much, because they hardly ever tell each other the truth. Maybe they stick to the insights of Habermas, whose central theme is the 'communicative action', the 'communicatively socialized subjects' and the 'unlimited communicative community'. It was a great progress, in that people came from 'subject-philosophical (Kant) to language-pragmatic understanding (Pierce) of the use of reason', but in order to get through to the truth, Habermas has to introduce and clarify quite a few additional terms: there must be mutual approximations and obligations, moral learning processes and much more must take place in order to reach the great 'We', which can then have the consent of all. An immense philosophical conceptual apparatus frames the whole.[3]

That's true in a way, but can't it be simpler? Mechthild of Magdeburg has shown it, but her search for truth is for us today too much captured by the direct reference to God and an extreme self-sublimation. Lacan also conveys it directly when he says that language does not serve communication at all, but revelation, admission, self-disclosure. The philosophers do not reveal themselves, they do not give away their anxiety, they do not give away their innermost. They remain in the good, enormously far-reaching, profound thoughts that they have made for themselves. For the psychoanalyst, Habermas's 'acts of speech acts' are mental defense mechanisms that seek to circumvent the reports of one's own unconscious desire. Despite this, philosophers are interesting to read, but they do not bring the decisive point.

Precisely, it is about desire, about a driving force that cannot be resisted so easily. And it is the same with the power of love and death that no one knows exactly what is right, true and characteristic in them, although one must follow them exactly, necessarily, imperatively. Thereby it has always been disturbing that the love has mostly lost to the death. Even if for millennia a god or several gods should be a guarantor that it also works 'the

---

[3] Habermas, J., Also a history of philosophy, vol. 2, Suhrkamp (2019) pp. 750 - 785.

other way round', in that the life after death would continue in an otherworldly realm, the question remains about the complete ambiguity of this otherworldly life and its powers.

What is love about? Doesn't it always pass away in the same way, no matter how much it is sung about? "Love is as strong as death," says the Song of Songs, [4] and in many other places it is added that God loves more than human beings could ever do. But for this one must "prove faithful even unto death", and moreover it is monotonously asserted that anyway "love is the greatest", etc., etc. [5] A continuous, meaningless talk. In other words, it is actually about a bet that is constantly made and that one always has to make again, in order to somehow successfully smuggle oneself over questionable issues of death and love. It is about the 'other way round' of love and death, because in normal use one always confuses these forces with negative consequences.

Because even if there is to find a grain of truth at all the normal around said, for the today's science culture these somewhat sweepingly exaggerated truths are not sufficient any more. One must convey that 'the other way round' in a new and provable form, so that one must no longer only believe, but can also have an authentic knowledge of it. More than hundred years ago psychoa-

---

[4] The Song of Songs 8; 6
[5] Revelation 2; 10 and 1Co 13, 13

nalysis started with the 'other way round'. The main part of the soul is - 'other way round' than conscious - in the so-called unconscious, which is the reservoir of repressed or even completely split off emotions and meanings.

But with regard to love and death of all things, psychoanalysis has stumbled a bit, in my opinion precisely because of the lack of the 'visionary'. The literary critic E. Goebel thought that above all Freud's death drive hypothesis is to blame for the fact that the psychoanalytic overall concept ultimately turns out to be pessimistic.[6] This is because the active eros-life drives have no chance in the face of death. Death is therefore described by the French psychoanalyst J. Lacan as the "absolute master" whom no way passes, and in love he sees - along with hate and ignorance - a form of nothingness.

Before I continue with the fact that the nothing is not logically conceivable without a something, the one only exists against the background of the zero and the existence can only be imagined against the background of a non-existence, and thus these statements cancel and balance each other out a bit, something personal: As a doctor I have always asked myself why people waste so much time and energy in order not to die of a disease. They take tons of medications, constantly consider one surgery or another, and seek so-called second and third opinions

---

[6] Goebel, E., Beyond the discomfort, transcript (2009) S. 10 -14

for everything, but with little progress. Wouldn't it be better 'the other way round' to use death as something instrumentally helpful, to acquire a 'diaita' (δίαιτα), a special way of life or art of living, as the ancient Greeks called it. Diaita' was theory and practice and went beyond philosophy.

I myself suffer from a somatoform pain disorder, which is bearable and from which one can by no means die. It is a constant companion that disturbs, but which after years has developed more and more into a life compass. That is, I feel when something is not good for me, I have taken on, behaved wrongly or nourished myself. Through this I don't think about death anymore, on the contrary, I have developed exactly from these guidelines, from this rea-son, the method which I have announced in the subtitle and which can be learned exactly in the sense of this compass by everyone himself. A method of self-aware-ness and self-therapy, to adhere to a 'diaita', from which, of course, the word diet is derived, but also precisely other artful soul and body techniques, is in the final anal-ysis nothing new. I will come back to it in detail by scien-tifically justifying the mentioned new procedure, which I have called *Analytic Psychocatharsis*.

Back to the nothing, to the zero, to the fundamental lack, which - following Lacan - has made the actual beginning, even if one has to think of the corresponding background of being to it. That one has spoken of the big bang as a beginning of the universe, is only correct in a subordinate sentence and has taken place only on a side stage. If one starts from a science from the subject, whose object is in each case oneself, the beginning lies much more in the relevance, which can be grasped only in each individual practically and not in a generalized theory. The philosopher G. Simmel spoke in this respect of the "individual law", in which the individual receives an object-relevance in himself.[7] For when I write and narrate here, everything starts with an 'I speak, therefore I am'. It begins and ends with the "l'etre parlant" as Lacan named the human being in his basic function and then formulated this function almost up to a psychoanalysis completely 'the other way round', i.e. a self-analysis.[8]

And so to begin with nothing is to begin wrongly as usual. Kant, for example, began with the question of 'synthetic judgments a priori' by claiming that there are analytic judgments which are automatically true a priori, because they are already contained, so to speak, in the rules of language we use when we use, for example, the word use: Usefulness ist useful - an analytic judgment, a priori true. But it is also somehow nonsensical and banal. Kant admits this nonsense, but now grabs the synthetic judgments (which are therefore not already conditioned

---

[7] Simmel, G., Complete Edition (1995)

[8] Lacan's 17th seminar 'L'envers de la Psychanalyse', has been translated as 'The other side of psychoanalysis', but it is actually about the 'other way round' of psychoanalysis, about a psychoanalysis upside down.

by the rules of language) and then starts to fill whole books with the truths which he now obtains by a syllogism of the analytic with the synthetic judgments.[9]

Thus, he can then easily begin with the word begin: actively the cause begins (in fit), he says, because passively beginning as causality becomes cause (fit).Now he does not need to ask why in the word causation he already prefigures the cause (makes it, so to speak, primordial). In short: in this way he comes to be the philosopher of his time, the professor, the university teacher, the knower.[10] He says everything right, he knows everything exactly - and this is quite true also for today and for all other sciences - but Kant does not say it well enough! Not in such a way that one could experience it directly. Everything is rightly known, but not well communicated, not well conveyed, not well said! (It was already so in Kant's time that the readers groaned over his works).

After all, Kant would like it if, as Lacan suggests, one would start with the lack, the zero, and speak of the 'exsistent', in that something 'sists' (persists) 'ex' (outside). A God, for example, which then - as in the case of my catholic old people's home sisters - does not really exist anymore, because one finds him only in the 'ex', where he persists. The Catholic philosopher of religion R. Spae-

---

[9] Indeed, the word 'judgment' often implies something very different in both cases.

[10] Kant, I., Critique of Pure Reason, Reclam (1993) p. 499.

mann therefore said that God is an "immortal rumor". This was not meant negatively. A Someone who is and will always be spoken of is better than the image of an old man with a beard or even than constant cathechetic repetitions. So it is about someone who does not exist within the here and now, but who nevertheless can have body, but it is a body without shape, without form, just 'ex'.

The modern philosopher of consciousness T. Metzinger ascribes to man a 'phenomenal self-model', i.e. an independent ego, a conscious-feeling inner perspective, which Lacan also calls an 'imaginary object'.[11] Metzinger starts from the horror of suffering, into which to look leads to the fact that it also looks into oneself, as Nietzsche said.[12] But real suffering can only be felt and correctly assessed in oneself and then also in others, who fulfills further criteria than an 'imaginary object', than a firmly delineated ego-feeling in oneself. One needs a 'suffering metric', Metzinger thinks, in order to be able to really understand suffering in its quantity and quality, but the philosopher has to reach far out in order to be able to write about how suffering could now really be reduced and how one would then no longer have to speak only of consciousness, but of Awareness, of Compassion-Awareness.

---

[11] Metzinger, T., In the Ocean of Agony, SZ, 23. 4. 2021.
[12] Nietzsche, F., Beyond Good and Evil, DTV (1999).

Metzinger also sees the difference between the imaginary and the symbolic objects, that is, between the perspective, phenomenal order of the conscious living being oriented to appearance and image on the one hand. On the other hand the order oriented to the word , to the symbol, to the comprehensive world of language, which, for example, can also lead to the fact that one can suffer terribly from a loss of dignity. Even the whole mankind, he thinks, could suffer from lack of dignity and perish, if climate and environmental factors are not brought under control. For the expanded consciousness, which thus already pushes towards consciousness by including compassion and co-awareness, references to the complexity of language and speech are thus also necessary.

However, I do not start from a political or neuro-philosophical consideration, but from a psychological, psychoanalytical, unconsciously spiritual one. In their sense one must likewise distinguish consciousness from awareness. The latter can still be present in the half-dead state, as one could determine with so-called near-death experiences. The person lying in a kind of unconsciousness can see himself as if from the outside and also grasp this holistically, but is not awake-conscious. Something similar exists with the 'Déjà Vu', the convincingly strong sensation to have experienced something exactly like this before. There is no consciousness, but a naive consciousness, which can be clarified even further in a psychoanalysis, because behind the 'Déjà Vu' there is a 'Jamais Raconte', a never told, repressed, classical case of a completely 'other way round'.

But the mystical ecstatic is also far detached from consciousness in his rapture, he is often outwardly barely awake and yet is in a kind of awareness. Here the phenomenon of awareness without consciousness becomes perhaps even clearer. I remember the well-known Indian saint Ramakrishna, who sometimes had to be brought back from his rapture by force, so kataton, frozen, drifted off, he seemed in his meditations. Certainly, the closeness to mental illness can be felt here, but only with a reference to mental extremes one does not do justice to awareness.

In order not to suffocate in boring theory, I want to bring an example from my own application of the *Analytic Psychocatharsis*, which can bring clarity into the psychological and psychoanalytical from another side. I start from the Freudian unconscious, to which the same applies, namely one does not find it in one's own consciousness, because it is 'ex' of oneself and yet at the same time the most inner.In order to discover this and to keep it going permanently, just as the vestal virgins in ancient Rome were never allowed to let the fire go out, today an increasingly large team of neuroscientists, spiritual scientists and psychoanalysts is needed. I want to give this 'ex', back to each individual, because only the individual can achieve true awareness, which requires a practice of which an ounce is worth more than a ton of theories, as the old saying goes. Theorists, philosophers and consciousness researchers were sublime hysterics for Freud; they try to establish the truth about being, man, love, death, etc. only out of themselves by screwing up their own thougths.

When I once again practiced the procedure, which thus combines meditative and psychoanalytic methodology, I noticed after about an hour of such a concentration exercise not only a clear relaxation, but also a physically perceptible concentration in the center of the body, which developed upwards beyond the head as if into an ever higher 'mountain', which was also visually visible in an implied way. Apart from a certain mightiness (not power) of this image, this imaginary impression, I also found myself in an extremely pleasant state and at the same time in some kind of certainty of having reawakened an ancient symbol.

This 'mountain experience' seemed to have been very close to the body, 'bodily' as one used to say. Physically perceptible. So it was about a relation to the unconscious more on the level of unconscious bodily images, while in conventional psychoanalysis the level of unconscious phrases is more in the foreground, which is why Lacan says: "It speaks in the unconscious". But this projected inward, the somatoform of my experience, transmitted itself like an It Feels, It Radiates, It Chills.[13] The body images are unconscious, but just 'bodily' aspects, which have the same importance as the mentioned unconscious phrases.

Thus, as a psychoanalyst, I know that this 'mountain' can also be interpreted as a phallic symbol, as the usual phrase, the word-acting of the 'phallus symbolique', as Lacan constantly called Id (this heraldic figure of Freud's Id) in his psychoanalytic seminars.[14] My 'mountain' had, however, besides the heraldic symbolic also something imaginary-real (figuratively corporeal) about it. For it was not - or not essentially - a memory or a fantasy articulating a phallic desire, but something a bit more substantial, image-acting, 'vision'-like. With a reference to Freud's science I can distinguish this description fully from earlier representations in mysticism, religion, yoga or by today's esotericists. Because I will specify my 'mountain experience' in reference to picture-scientific and psychoanalytical procedures. Above all I will con-

---

[13] It has something to do with the physical 'trickling through', which one knows from deep emotionality, e.g. when listening to a moving piece of music. That's why I also call it an Id Rays, Id Shows, Id Shines.

[14] Many do not understand what a symbolic phallus should be. It means, symbolizes sexual desire. When the French Minister of Justice R. Dati spoke of fellatio instead of inflation, it was clear that this repressed signifier, symbolic signifier (and not predominantly real or imaginary) had intervened here.

nect this Rays-phenomenon with that of Id Speaks, whereby a scientific consolidation is achieved.

Thus, I already depict down here such a formula-word, which is used in the first meditative exercise of the *Analytic Psychocatharsis* and which I have also used in the example with the 'mountain'. It contains several meanings in a single (here written in a circle) stroke.[15] The meanings overlap, so that the writing as such does not say anything, there is an 'overdetermination' (multiple statement), as it is known from the psychoanalytic dream interpretation. But this is just advantageous, because in this way the unconscious, which is purely structurally built up in the same way as the formula-word, is irritated, provoked and awakened to give out its, and that means

now also unconsciously my, me concerning, meaning (for which a second exercise will serve).

Because I attribute only a casual meaning to my 'mountain experience'. For me, this 'appearance', this imaginary-real, 'vision'-like, is only a small part of my process. The felt, 'chilling' 'mountain' only represents something cathartic, that is, a liberating, purifying, purely figurative-real, clarifying experience, which does not allow any precise statement. In Freud's theory, I would classify such an experience close to the place that Freud called introductory-

---

[15] Contents and details of the formula word in Chapter 3.

representation. There the driving force - here now that of the perceptual or visual drive - is directly psychically represented, which from there usually leads to an uncontrolled affect or to defense mechanisms (if the drive is not endured and is shifted into complex thinking or into symptoms).

Nevertheless, this part, which is more related to the imaginary-real, to the image-acting, is important. It even represents the main part of the book, because in classical psychoanalysis only or quite emphasized, the symbolic-real, the word-acting comes into play. Lacan clearly recognized this and tried to give shape to the pictorial, the imaginary significant (imaginary-real) with geometrical figures, topologies, knot formations and braid-like representations. But even with this he remained far behind the gravity of the word-acting. To experience the image-acting itself, to have a kind of 'vision', even almost to be able to communicate with it, has something great about it, which one cannot completely sweep under the table.

Also someone who has climbed several eight-thousanders or who has scaled spiritual and mathematical heights may have a quite comparable 'mountain experience', which just like mine is not the last word in wisdom. But leaning back after reaching the summit and having the feeling of floating above everything may correspond exactly to the imaginary-real. The simultaneously physical and spiritual, the mental climax, fulfills as an event the Freudian drive-structure-concept with its starting-, object-, and target-dynamics in a different and yet again the same way, mainly directed to the image-acting. One is seized by a 'vision', which almost corresponds to an act of love.

In later chapters I will go into more detail about how Lacan places love exactly in this context with the image-acting. He does not want to follow the usual bla bla with which it is talked, written and filmed in human relations, but also in the spiritual or elsewhere. He does not want to perform a tricky plot like the director M. Haneke in his film 'Love', in which an old man devotedly cares for his equally old, demented wife, but in the end presses a pillow on her face. Indeed, from the title to all the gestures, Haneke suggests to his viewers that this so-called 're-demptive gesture' conveys the climax, indeed the very love 'the other way round'. But it isn't true. As I have argued in more detail elsewhere, the man cruelly, pitiless-ly suffocates his wife. He himself is portrayed as a par-ticularly loving nurturer, but he is a narcissist, he has overwhelmed himself, and the gesture of love is per-verse.[16]

In contrast, Lacan's love is the tissue behind the psycho-analytic act, almost invisible and also not sayable, be-cause the transference love that occurs in psychoanalysis is neurotic. The patient transfers unconscious meanings to the therapist in a positive, loving way, but this process

---

[16] Hummel, G., v. Outsmarting death two times, BoD (2021)

is inadequate; the transference has nothing to do with the real (word-acting) relationship between therapist and patient. As transference, it results from the assumption that the therapist has the knowledge of what the patient is about specifically also the knowledge of true enjoyment. As I have argued in more detail elsewhere, the man cruelly, pitilessly suffocates his wife. Transference / assumption, the former is related to the word-acting, the latter to the image-acting, there is a swinging movement. With the love of the 'mountain experience' it is no different, though not as neurotic. It simply behaves more 'visionary', which is also not harmless.

So it is about an 'other way round' of love, about its seductive, exciting imaginary-real, image-acting, which also corresponds to an 'other way round' of death. This, in turn, has its emphasis in the symbolic-real, in the word-acting, because - as Freud argued - it realized its climax in the murder of the father, in that the sons envied him the women.[17] Later, they would have repented of this act and, out of guilt, would have elevated the father to the rank of a god. This is correct and logical, however, I have a 'other way round' version of the death. The great important father figure was not murdered, but negated and forgotten.

---

[17] Freud, S., Totem und Tabu, GW IX, Fischer (2001)

Rather, it was so that over many generations stories of him were told on and on. In the process, however, reality faded and he was thus raptured into the afterlife and was considered never to have died completely. One did not have to raise this father out of guilt, but out of shame about the fact that one disregarded him more and more and forgot his image and his look. For love and death there is, so to speak, a normal and an 'other way round'. In the normal, death is always the companion of all stories, while love conveys the content. 'Other way round', however, they produce a kind of this now already repeatedly discussed consciousness, soulfulness, which in former times could only be expressed by letting the lovers be united only in death, as for example in Verdi's opera Aida or Puccini's Tosca.

As is well known, Freud had begun to treat patients with hypnosis. He sent them into an apparent death, from where they remembered repressed things and could make speeches about them without inhibitions, shamelessly, so to speak. But the patients enjoyed this state of regression into the earliest phases of life, they put themselves into the fulfilled consciousness, and again awakened from hypnosis they did not really want to know anything more about what they had remembered from the unconscious. Finally, Freud wanted to distance himself from this primary enjoyment to which the patients gave themselves in dependence on his hypnotizing voice. The cathartic trance - he thought - led the patients too far away from the therapeutic process, and so he abandoned hypnosis in favor of the openly symbolic, the verbally active. Freud had his patients speak 'freely associating' from the outset, as spontaneously as possible, as if they were in a trance.

By spontaneously expressing themselves, the patients remained more mature, more conscious, more serious, and could no longer evade unconscious truths in such a deprecating way. They could trivialize the scenes of themselves seen in hypnosis (it was only a movie, they said), but in the messed-up speaking of 'free association' the references to the unconscious, even if distorted, emerged in such a way that they could be consciously discussed. They only had to be bent or interpreted a bit rightly by the therapist. But the wonderful catharsis in which the patients could bathe themselves no longer existed.

I interpret Freud's approach to be that hypnosis was about a love the 'other way round' that made a deal with death (the like apparent dead in hypnosis). In the rapturous realm of pleasures, even death was a placeholder for love. In the semi-awake state of hypnosis, the patients were close to drifting away, to letting themselves fall as if into death, and had no problem recalling the early childhood drive events and bathing themselves in lascivious feelings of love. The closer they came to the "bliss of death" which, according to Lacan, "always exists in love," the more they loved, the more they became excited, and even the more they fell for the sound of the therapist's fatherly voice.[18]

Later, after leaving hypnosis and arriving at psychoanalysis, or its classical form, reason triumphed. Death became again what it always was, the - as mentioned - pessimistic part of life, in which love led only a shadowy existence. Neither therapist nor patient may have stronger feelings of love, because absolute neutrality is prescribed. It is allowed to talk about love, but dying in it, fulfillment of awareness, is not allowed.

.In the procedure of *Analytic Psychocatharsis*, however, I use the liberating, beatific catharsis in a different sense, in which it is used constructively, thus bringing the 'other way round' back in a new form. The catharsis is a 'l'amourire' as Lacan says, a dying love, which is considered a prerequisite for the occurrence of the pass-words. These are words that come from the unconscious when the procedure is applied, stimulated by the formula-words, and that crown the process of this self-analysis by leading to a definitive statement.[19] For me, the catharsis not only promotes the imaginary, image-acting, but by its stimulating radiance, by its awareness-filling, leads in

---

[18] Lacan, J. The Transference, Seminar VIII, session of 5/15/61, where Lacan adds that "there is the delight of death in love only when it is not self-imposed."

[19] The pass-words are not that what is called in the computer language. On the contrary, they are formulations from the unconscious, which help to express one's own identity.

concentrated form to the symbolic, if one gives it a scientifically founded guidance.

For the symbolic from the unconscious, that is, that which speaks in the unconscious itself, can be brought out, for example, much better than by 'free association' and interpretation (also of dreams) by the direct impulse or initiation by means of the formula-words. The formula-words themselves say nothing, as mentioned, they only initiate the symbolization process. But they do this only in elementary-linguistically structured form, and more is not necessary. They should not only be word-acting, but also image-acting, in order to challenge the likewise built-up unconscious. They should not suggest anything, not merely promote consciousness. [20]

Thus I have taken a step in the direction with which psychoanalysis has always struggled. With its main emphasis on language and speech, the word-acting, it has to compensate for the lack of the image-acting by linguistic constructs: by so-called 'enactments', by countertransferences, and by interpretive constructions, all measures that do not follow the otherwise necessary logic of language. Lacan tried to compensate for this deficiency, as mentioned, by geometrical drawings, topologies and cord

---

[20] Already the philosopher M. Heidegger said, "Language speaks in man". Lacan condensed this to a "Cà parle dans l'inconscient', It speaks in the unconscious.

meshes, which I will now briefly discuss and thus interpret my 'mountain' as not quite so unimportant after all.

A short dwelling in the imposing event of this kind of 'vision is worth a lot, even if it still has to be completed - as announced - by such a pass-word. But then it shortens the long talking around of the conventional psychoanalytic session, even if it is very interesting and intellectually rich. It is not very conducive to healing anyway, as Freud said. Well, maybe it is not always so pronounced in *Analytic Psychocatharsis* either.

2. Lacan's Triple Braid

As already reported, Lacan starts from the fundamental trinity of the imaginary, image-acting, then the symbolic, word-acting, and finally the real, and represented this in the construction of his Borromean Knot (abbreviated Bo-Knot). It is a model of the human soul, which can split just as the knot unravels when only one of the three loops (and thus their areas) is severed or unraveled.[21] The figure below shows all possible references, but it is not necessary to know all of them in every detail. Imaginary and symbolic together produce the sense, as it is best shown

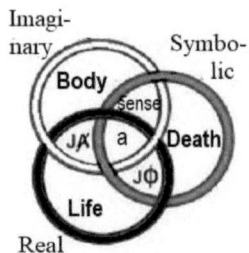

by the writing. Life as such, the vital, belongs to the real by conveying what is always in its place. For it is without crack, without structure. It is the life always working behind all reality.

But back to the 'mountain', which in my experience took place between the imaginary and the real, because it had something vital (life) about it, but was also physically tangible. Thus, the enjoyment that Lacan calls JA, 'jouissance de l'Autre', plays a crucial role. L'Autre, the Other, by Lacan also through the al-

---

[21] I use the ancient word soul and not the modern psyche to express the encompassing of the conscious and the unconscious.

ready quoted "çà parle dans l'inconscient" (It speaks in the unconscious), to which - according to Freud - a knowledge without calculation, thinking or calculating belongs. It is not one's own knowledge, but this knowledge from the unconscious of his patient that the psychoanalyst needs, it is for this, namely that it some- how appears in dreams, slips of the tongue, and associa- tions, that the psychoanalyst must strive. L'Autre, the Other, is not perfect (hence the slash in the A), the inter- nalizations of parents, caregivers, teachers up to the ana- lyst have contributed to its emergence inside each person and are thus unconsciously hidden in it. Now he/it, l'Au- tre, can appear, however, not only speaking but also fig- uratively in the form of a 'mountain' as I claim.

Because to experience the 'mountain' I could use the Bo-Knot Lacan wrapped into a braid - triple braid he calls it (fig. aside).[22] It is the exact same intertwining of the three categori- cal loops, strands, cords as in the Bo knot, and after a six fold knotting they have returned to the starting position with small a in the middle. Small a represents the (psychic) object of de- sire, which can be differently constituted each time, as the oral, for example, i.e., as the mouth lust, which the gourmet develops into the paranoia

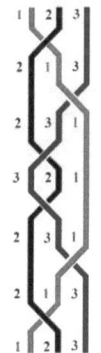

---

[22] Lacan, J., Seminar XXI, lecture of 12. 3. 1974, Staferla free, where the illustration is also shown.

of the palate tickle, or as the gaze in my 'mountain'. Now the look, the appearance of the 'mountain' just like the other mentioned 'mountain experiences' would indeed not be worth much, if it would not have come into being by a special effort, art or as in my case by the fact that I could produce it with the braid of the formula word. For the formula-word has, after all, also been wound from different meanings - linguistically, so to speak - exactly structurally the same, like Lacan's triple braid.

Lacan's braid reminds a bit of Münchausen's braid, with which the latter could pull himself out of the swamp. And indeed, to be able to meditatively pull oneself out of the unconscious by means of overlapping phrases and into the height of a 'mountain' sounds similar, but is something quite different. I will come back to this in detail, because otherwise I would have already given away almost everything what this book is about. All in all, however, the 'mountain' still has no logically secured message, just as little as Münchhausen's flight of fancy. There is no Id Speaks of the A to be written large, of l'Autre, of the Other in it; the 'mountain' is not enough word-acting, mature symbolic, but only appearance, image-acting, even if it is - as the philosopher W. Seitter said - an appearance with meaning, with impressive, authoritative.[23] Id Rays / Speaks, however, not sufficiently

---

[23] Seitter, W., Physics of existance, Sonderzahl (1997) pp. 213-14.

definitely. But perhaps approximately, preparing, suggesting and above all strongly impacting.

At this point, in fact (and especially in the twenty-first seminar), Lacan introduces the reference to love and death, because love, too, is nothing that can be said definitively, while with death everything already appears perfectly articulated. Death always wants to have the last word and would get it, were it not for love 'the other way around', which exploits its tendency to retreat, its inclination to regression, its addiction to darkness and all these things in order to be able to unfold. Love 'the other way around' needs the passionate, but also the suffering hiding places, the states of absorption, the light absences and fainting, as well as the image-working of consciousness, the very great aesthetics.

Freud started from the libido as a force that can bind itself to its own ego or to objects outside, and only such a successful balance of "ego libido and object libido" Freud calls love. That was a bit poor. Where are the excitations about the very great lovers of world literature, those of gods and goddesses, of forbidden and suppressed loves, or even those of a lustful creator of it all? Where are the death longings of hopelessly manic lovers, where are those of hermits immersed in love for a lifetime, and above all those of the 'visionaries', the wisdom showers and prophets of the future? They were all enraptured, infatuated and as if intoxicated in the look for the 'other way round' of love and death. For the love no science is responsible except the aesthetics, the image-view-acting, the Rays in its fullness. This even includes death.

In psychoanalysis, only words are spoken. It is tried to decode the words, even if they are twisted and nonsensical, to the point of no longer being able to be decoded from the unconscious and exchanged between patient and therapist as the main medium. But it remains with the word. Symbolic in low connection to the real dominates the field in which JΦ, the 'jouissance phallique' (Φ, Greek letter Phi as abbreviation) is the decisive pivot. There is seemingly no place reserved for love in the Bo-Node, and yet the node is surrounded by a fluidum of an amorous kind, because one must love it if one wants to experience, recognize and know oneself before death screws everything up. One must love it as a whole, so to speak, in its unreadability, that is, in its topological beauty.

This is exactly the point when I say that psychoanalysis lacks the image-acting, the 'visionary' or the - as I will define it later - ironical. I have already mentioned that Lacan tried to do some justice to the image-acting with the figures, the loop formations and overturnings of topology. But he remains in theory. Today nobody dares to jump directly into the shamelessness of looks, images and forms as the 'seers', the mystics, the visionaries did in former times, because - admittedly - too many are stranded with it. Especially for this reason one has started to do science. However, the so-called image science is a sober, sad, equally purely theoretical stuff. One needs practice.

That in my 'mountain' so impressively picture-acting and real can certainly be understood only with difficulty in the conventional psychoanalysis. But I will justify it more comprehensibly. For the time being it must suffice that the 'mountain experience' was so fantastic that I must speak of it. And I also had to stop it after a short time, because it was clear to me that one can also completely lose oneself in such 'visions', if one attaches too much value to them. Now the 'mountain' visualized by me was not dry theory or topology, but just close to life, it moved a little, it grew, it made happy. Love was there, but without fulfilling clarity, without confirming headline, without truth check, without fulfilling awareness - at least for the moment.

Even if the 'mountain experience' is only episodic and entirely subject-related, the directness of the experience can nevertheless keep up well with the theory. It is an equally secure piece of evidence, is confirmation and certainty. It becomes clearer and clearer that both are needed next to and with each other: the word-acting Speaks and the image-acting Rays. And it cannot be achieved alone in the classical situation of speaking on the couch, but it must be used in an additional practical exercise. For this, the therapist is only needed in the background or hardly at all.

It is often only a hindrance anyway. Lacan thought that the therapist rather than the patient is responsible for the well-known resistance to revealing the truth in the therapeutic procedure. If he coughs at the wrong time, clears his throat or moves strongly, says something too early or inappropriately, his voice seems threatening and he disturbs above all with his countertransference, this also disturbs the therapy.[24] In the end, however, it is the combination of the two basic elements (Rays/Speaks) that is decisive in practice, and there the Rays of the 'mountain' belong to it as well as the Speaks of its meaning. I will discuss this important point several times. Because all authors in philosophy and psychoanalysis have only arguments, but do not enable the real bringing together in practice.

The classical psychoanalyst will nevertheless not fully recognize my argumentation. He will say, for example, that certainty can also be delusional, paranoid. I do not want to exclude this completely. But already the well-known surrealistic painter S. Dali spoke of his 'paranoic-critical method' as a way of interpretation of his art in the sense of a realization of

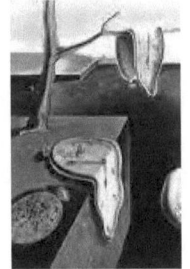

---

[24] The countertransference is a reaction of the psychoanalyst to what the patient transfers to him in terms of meanings. It does not consist in logically derived interpretations, but in intuitively expressed thoughts of the therapist.

unconscious mental processes. For example, the image of his waxy watches, which he titled 'The permanence of memory', is usually understandable without this title. As the image detail beside shows, time does not pass as linearly as the usual material clocks would like to convey to us. Depending on shortness and boredom, depending on haste and apathy and still more according to Einstein depending on criteria of space-time they can vary very much.

Time is waxy - paranoiac-critical in Dali's and Einstein's sense said. Now this does not change the fact that there is also the apparently linear time, which is so determining for our today's culture. One must always bring the two times together. The certainty, the memory, the image, the Rays, the imaginary in general, are not scientific proofs. They are only enormously important for the support of the word-acting, the speaking, that is, both must support each other, and with it one gets past the paranoia in the best way. But this problem also exists in classical psychoanalysis.

If I consider the imaginary-real on its own and just as my own 'mountain experience' as isolated critical for use in *Analytic Psychocatharsis*, the same criticism applies to psychoanalysis. Since there one relies only on the word-acting, and what is transferred to the therapist is inadequate, one speaks of transference neurosis, i.e. an artificially set neurosis. This neurosis must then be eliminated by giving appropriate transference interpretations. That sounds rather complicated. If there is something artificial in my 'mountain experience', then there is also something artificial in the single-sided speaking in the transference to the therapist. Nevertheless, both steps are justified, because in both cases one does not remain completely with the single-sidedness, but rather with the One-sidedness, in which the One as Unum purum is the focal point.

Again: because of this artificiality in psychoanalysis, this lack of the image-acting in it, which leads to the mentioned 'enactments' and interpretative constructs, the psychoanalyst H. Will has described so-called 'micro regressions'.[25] Therapist and patient should regress together, that is, fall back into earlier or more elementary states of soul together. One should be able to dream together, become playful, silly together, and the like. Will also quotes A. Ferro, an Italian and somewhat outsider psychoanalyst who has long spoken of the 'pensiero onirico della veglia' (waking dream thinking).[26] Ferro, too, indulges in this waking dream thinking with his patient and then tries to draw rational conclusions from what they have experienced together 'oneirically' (dreamlike). But for this one

---

[25] Will, H., Regression zum Träumen (Regression to Dreaming), PSYCHE No. 7 (2021) pp. 561 - 591. Regression means return to more elementary states of psychic development.

[26] Ferro, A., Pensieri di uno psicoanalista irriverente, Raffaelo Cortina (2017)

must collect many such 'pensieri onirici della veglia', many in many therapy hours, which makes the matter not only dreamlike, but also lengthy and expensive. In the *Analytic Psychocatharsis*, the waking dream thinking is already controlled, pre-controlled, by the extremely formal of the formula words.

Ultimately, it is about the same as in my Id Rays/Speaks, namely about the image-acting, the imaginary-real, so culpably neglected in psychoanalysis, for which Will now seeks compensatory paths. But how they finally lead to the clearly symbolically expressed contents is not quite clear, similar to Ferro. Although Will emphasizes that the contact to the repressed is facilitated, the emotional processing function of the analyst is stimulated and also the symbolization (wording) is initiated, this all sounds just as vague as my 'mountain'. For this also allows processing functions in the psychoanalytic process, whereby these even lead much more directly to concrete symbolizations, namely through the mentioned pass-words, to which it had not come in my example with the 'mountain' now. However, I will make up for this in the following example.

This other example for the thus more to the image-acting, to the Rays belonging, one of my adepts, who practiced the *Analytic Psychocatharsis* already for a longer time, has recently experienced. Waking up from a dream - so he reported - he would have perceived for a short time, perhaps for a few seconds, a fixed, thus rigidly remaining image, which touched him somehow strongly (see the picture of a tree painted by me exactly according to his information on the right). So it was no longer a dream, but a kind of 'vision' similar to the mentioned 'mountain'. I do not deny the relation of the term 'vision' to the real, but it  is often too much dominated by denomination, prefabricated instructions or ideas. The 'vision' exactly at the point of the drive representation, however, leads immediately to the realization and revelation and thus the purpose of the drive and can thus be understood psychoanalytically differently.

In the case of the 'tree vision' it seemed to have been almost the reverse, something immobile, but for that it stood out all the better from the violently moving dream. I see in it the same mechanism, namely to want to give the image-acting, the imaginary-real from Lacan's knot, an elementary structured bodily life, a pictorial ordering potency (again no power, but a strengthening, consolidation of the soul). For while the dream quickly passes one by, even staggering along, this remaining, this insistence of an image as exhibited or emphatically shown, of the truly image-working, had a slightly beguiling, seeming and stabilizing effect on the aforementioned adept.

Here obviously something is to be imparted to him, here not quickly the dream program is played through, but something of it - however absolutely not uncontrolled, but guided and supported by the formula-word in the meditation - is brought out. It was thus the opposite of the smooth visual communication in the form of pictures, but also of the too lexically ordered language. Admittedly, the painted image obscures the authenticity of the real, unless it could be considered as great art. But here, in the exercises of the *Analytic Psychocatharsis*, it depends on the directly experienced imaginary-real, to which I emphasize that only the individual can experience the truth of his identity - in real time and in real space - even if additionally supported by the symbolic (formula- and in this case by the pass-word to be discussed in a moment).

My adept had immediately the impression that the oversized sphere-like formations were fruits of the tree, but seemed like artificially somewhere from outside sent perfectly round spheres. More soul-spiritual (spheres) and more biological-natural (tree) should perhaps be shown connected in this way, he himself thought, and he felt this like a reminder, revelation and heraldic destiny, because at the last moment he thought he had heard the expression 'Mene'. 'Mene'? Or did it not sound like `Mine'? Both made sense to him and was therefore a real password concerning which I will give still further examples and explanations. For certainly it had to do with his 'Mene Tekel', a quite personal interpretation, which I will not elaborate here for data protection reasons.

But already the consistency, the short but somehow also stubborn lingering of the picture, seems a bit like a 'Mene Tekel'. Just like the consistenc of the image, the insistence of the letters now also makes up the power of the unconscious drive, thus its existence.[27] What manifested itself here more strongly from the viewing instinct as primarily as a vision-like imaginary-real, can express itself just as well from the speech instinct as primary-language, as original sound of the unconscious, as quite primary logical automatism, as It Id Rays/Speaks.[28]

I renounce here also Freudian interpretations about which I have spoken with the mentioned adept. He was a biology teacher and art lover. The art of the painter but also that of the 'visionary' is an elaborated form of the image-acting, as well as a philosophical treatise, but also mature, successful poetry is the elaborated form of the word-acting. The artist senses the primary, image-acting drive, he senses the radiance stimulating in him, and then translates it into his figurative or abstract painting technique through his self-developed art form, which is called his style here. However, one escapes the horror of the art market only, through the self-aesthetics of awareness.

---

[27] With figurative-imaginary consistence, wordlike-symbolic insistence, the existence of the real and thus the essence of the entire Bo knot thus also comes into play here.

[28] Lacan, J., Seminaire XVIII, 5. Lecture

Not differently the philosopher, who takes up the logical automatism in himself and realizes it with pure, always further increased thought labor to an elaborated, mental work. And the psychoanalyst? He proceeds in a similar way as the philosopher, only that he takes up what is spoken in a different way in himself (equally floating attentive listening) and in his patient (freely associated), in order to bring it into an elaborated interpretation.

So it also needs the Id Rays. In my experience I brought the primary image-acting Rays also into a more elaborated result - into the 'mountain', the symbolic Olympus, the holy Kailash, for which I want to betray a clear name (pass-word) only later and speak in this respect only provisionally of 'vision'. If I don't have a name for it or maybe I don't want to, so because the elaborated result leans on the essence of interpretation in psychoanalysis, but the 'vision' in the *Analytic Psychocatharsis* adds something essential. Therein lies the necessary emphasis on praxis, which falls short in conventional psychoanalysis. Freud himself therefore thought that it is not at all well suited for therapy and rather serves only to find the truth.

Everybody has to give himself the right name, even if this process is facilitated in the *Analytic Psychocatharsis* by the so-called identity- or pass-words. With this I can already hint here that I can only offer the known help for self-help, and that the decisive 'other way round' must happen in each individual himself. I can only lead to the conviction by scientifically founded argumentation that there is a practice with which the essentials to love and death can be experienced in such an 'other way round' that there are no more doubts about what they mean and how to deal with them and how pass-words come into being.

Love ('other way round') can be left like this in its excited-ness. Even if one loves or must love the Nothing, it remains the supporting element of the image-acting, of the Two in Lacanian mathematics, of the symmetry of two lovers. Death ('other way round'), on the other hand, one learns to forget, because it is always seen far too soon as the absolute end. It is lost in the multiplicity of 'visions', it lives only from the letters with which it is called. For the not speaking living beings the death does not exist. Only with the 'other way round' of love and death, the primary enjoyment, the said 'jouissance', can find its way also with l'etre parlant , the speaking being.

The thesis of the science journalist S. Klein, which he formulates in his latest book, also fits in with this.[29] He describes as the most important of all qualities of life the essence of imagination and creativity, which already the primates themselves with their still small brains could bring to full bloom. It was connected with the original, the autochthonous enjoyment, and concerns exactly what

---

[29] Klein, S., Wie wir die Welt ändern (How we are changing the world), S. Fischer (2021).

I have quoted above with Metzinger's awareness, which is an awareness of compassion, empathy, with-being and with-loving. The 'other way round' of love and death, in fact, needs such a naive awareness. With too much brain, with too much mind, too much intellect, one can have neither the enjoyment nor this awareness.

Now the concept of mind is even more difficult to handle than that of awareness. One cannot make it as easy as the philosopher F. W. Hegel. For him the spirit was divided into three parts: as absolutely divine it stood at the very top, as subjectively human it was to be owned by the general people and as objective world spirit it was valid for Hegel himself who examined it objectively, scientifically. For the modern successful author A. Damasio also ants have spirit. Of course not the cultural or scientific spirit of man, but more a primary-biological, instinctive one.

But why then say spirit to it? Why doesn't he say love, which would be just as curious, but once somewhat differently, somewhat 'other way round' said. What he means, concerns the enormous neuronal network-like structure of the ant society, which make so complex community structures possible for the animals, which resemble well developed state formations. Admittedly, one can imagine calling this and similar multi-layered ways of life of animals a kind of mind because of their hierarchical and network-like structure.

But is this of any use? Hegel would rather speak of the instinctive organism of nature in the case of ants, and I would speak of this awareness 'other way round' instead of spirit, which will be the subject of this book. For the 'other way round' of this awareness is not only valid for co-love, which, by the way, Antigone, the daughter of Oedipus, also placed in the center of her life; it is also advantageous for death to see its 'other way round' as an expression of naive but fulfilling awareness. When Lacan says that the psychoanalyst should speak with the voice of a dead person, he means the same thing, in that it is about a voice without human sound, without precon-ceived meaning, about a voice of naive awareness in which love, death and enjoyment are short-circuited (on which I will give further explanations).

By most modern philosophers and scientific authors of other disciplines the term spirit is used mainly for the thoughtful. Thoughts take place in the mind or spirit, and they are predominantly word-bound, thus belong both in the conscious and in the unconscious to the word-acting. The image-acting on the other hand we count in the con-scious area to the imaginations or ideas, which one makes oneself just consciously of something. But there are also unconscious ideas, and it is these that Freud brought into play with the 'representation of ideas' as a first drive structure to be grasped. In my opinion, this image-acting, unconscious area refers exactly to what theologians still call spirit today. Well, why not, the image-view-acting is so diffuse, so rich, that one can grasp it in the end just only by means of the connection with the word-acting. It is the images that seduce us, and when they are paired with the wrong words, it leads to disaster. That's why I also have to ascend from the 'mountain' to pure, cathartic lucidity and to find the right pass-words for it.

3. Making a Feast

In his seminars, J. Lacan often proclaimed the phrase: "To love means to give what one does not have." It is meant again the banal loving, because even if one loves, how can one bring it across to the other, how can one reach, even be sure, that he has the equally weighted experience of love as oneself? And even in the case that there is something that could be considered as an assured experience of love, even as proof of love, from one to the other, surely this only proves a functioning logical system between the two, but does it really prove love as such, love per se? What the psychoanalyst means, then, when he says, "To love means to give what one does not have," is surely that in love one gives (ontologically gives) on a level, that is, on the level of a being where the other loves a having, so that one oneself almost does not have to give at all, which would be to have as a real being of love.

If the lover hints at a `lo . . .', the beloved has long since added a '. . ve', because the whole thing takes place high up in a kind of delirium.It takes place in the imaginary-symbolic, in the two Borromean rings that stand in for the meaning that is already there before it should be unraveled. It may be that above all the everyday being in love, the emotional love, the romantic loving contains such a loving. Finally, the rapturous loving, which one gives to the other, is indeed something that can be well described with a being without having or a having without being.

Because do we really give - like St. George, for example - half of our coat when it should be about love for our neighbor? Of our fur coat, for example? We give blankets, tents and powdered milk when there are disasters in the third world. But the girls in the Bosnian war not only dreamed of a warm blanket, but they cried for the picture from a Cartier magazine; they would have gladly renounced some blanket and tent just for trying on a dress from Armani or Dior! Those who have hunger hallucinations do not see a dry old piece of bread in front of them that would satisfy their hunger, but epicurean dishes, tables that bend with delicacies. Why don't we bring to the poor half of our sports and off-road cars, half of our electronic toys or designer furniture? That would be true love!

But Lacan paraphrased even further, proclaiming, "To give what one has would mean to make a feast." So our fur coats and dresses from Massimo Dutti would also not yet fully fulfill what love could really be about, because then there is no longer any talk of it at all. There must be something else. Now it is always delicate and difficult, often clumsy and misunderstood, when one then lifts up to a minstrel song or spiritual flight of fancy and conjures up a love that goes beyond everything and that would deserve the highest laurels. On the other hand, I would like to do something with the word love, if it succeeded to pull this imaginary-symbolic into the real and thus not only to give what one does not have, but what one is or at least what one clearly suggests to be (as one perhaps also 'sees' in my example with the 'mountain' (because I love him and he me to make a feast).

I often meet people, friends, relatives, other couples, and yet they never say what it is really about, what would concern me and them, what would satisfy the desire that confirms me or them, understands me or them. Even in my psychoanalyses I seldom get to the point that well confided, revealed, admitted - or even - that well kept silent. The case history of one of my patients, who said nothing or almost nothing for weeks and months, fits this. In the early days of psychoanalysis, therapists also kept silent in such a situation, but for a long time now one has been intervening with constructed interpretations, as I have already mentioned with the concept of enactment and microregressions. It is a pity, because in the silence of this 'other way round' winding kind there is often more saying than in the communicative, but also associative speaking.

In the case of this patient, the idea of staying with the old procedure came to my mind. For a long time we spoke nothing or only a few rather meaningless words. I was already quite desperate when I felt that my somatoform pain disorder that I mentioned was somehow changing, and so I had the feeling that something was also moving in the patient. I thought that she probably also had such an experience, but that she had not perceived it as con-sciously as I did with it, when I immediately knew: this is serious, this will stay, but I will be able to endure it. Such an experience of a psychological, break-in-like disturbance had probably already occurred with her at the beginning of her life, where one does not yet have clear memories or splits it away from oneself in the trauma.[30] But now she was close again.

I therefore said to her. "I think that it will help you if we both say nothing for a long time. For there must have been a very early physical spiritual gap, emptiness, an abyss with you, and no one was there to help bridge this gap. Not even sounds, touches and warmth were present, although someone was present, shadowy and statuesque, but just not real. And now, many years later, words would probably not suffice, even be disturbing."

With tears and sobs, she burst out that it was just like that, but if someone was there, sitting here just for her, that gap would be bridged. Other people often have to talk irrelevant things when they are embarrassed. "For you," I therefore said after a long time, "it is only important that someone is there just for you, this 'just for you' is enough and is better than some talking, which even takes up most of the time in psychoanalysis. Free association, but also interpretative constructions often rather disturb". Now a conversation about the early phas-

---

[30] Not every trauma remains the cause of mental disorders, some are successfully split off and stay away with a kind of inner, primary conviction.

es in her life came about after all, even if in between there was still a lot of silence and remained unresolved.

The psychoanalyst S. Leikert also wants to distinguish the conventional, and thus so matter-of-factly sober, love-less psychoanalysis, which is based on speech and language, from that which, while not preferentially based on silence, refers more to the semantics of perception, aesthetics and inward sensibility.[31] Leikert also speaks of "kinesthetic semantics," a theory of meaning derived from internal sensation and internal movement (from the Greek kineo, to move). Psychoanalyst R. Zwiebel also emphasizes this more meditative and cathartic side, which should be considered more extensively in psychoanalysis today. Zwiebel refers to Yoga and Zen and to Freud's self-observation and self-therapy, which was more about the inner perception, the inner meaning.[32] Freud could only analyze himself on the basis of his own inner perception, he was still loving, but then psychoanalysis drifted more and more into the cold scientific.

Through the free associative speaking of conventional psychoanalysis one never gets back to the earliest phase of life, which Lacan called that of the 'corps morcelée',

---

[31] Leikert, S., Schönheit und Konflikt, Umrisse einer allgemeinen psychoanalytischen Ästhetik (Beauty and Conflict, Outlines of a General Psychoanalytic Aesthetics), Psychosozial Verlag (2012).

[32] Zwiebel, R., Weischede, G., Neurosis and Enlightenment, Klett-Cotta (2009).

the dismembered body, in my nomenclature: the pieces of the still raw Rays / Speaks. The like bodily piecemeal are the elementary psycho-physical states or the bodily images, the figurative pieces of the infant psyche, which does not yet possess a coordinating ego. Initially, the child still lives almost entirely in the imaginary-real, for its whimpering has nothing yet to do with the symbolic. This imaginary-real, captured in the "basic rhythm of a first whimpering and its subsiding" in the infant, is not yet call, claim of the child to the other, to the mother for example. It is the immediate real, its pain, its sorrow, its suffering, because it has lost something essential of itself.[33] And not only the body of the mother, but also a large part of itself in the form of the placenta, for example (a piece of its awareness of being).

Something like this can also be experienced in the practice of *Analytic Psychocatharsis*. I have often observed in a meditation group with others, but also with myself, just in deeper contemplation, a short sigh of relief, an unconscious, automatic sigh. It is not a made, self-pitying sigh, but a short sigh coming from the depths, a barely audible relief that emerges directly from the real. Obviously it has something to do with a regression into the earliest childhood, which is important for the opening of the un-

---

[33] Lacan, J., Seminar II, Walter (1980) p. 327. In psychoanalysis, the mother is considered the primary significant other who - internalized - also contributes to the formation of the first, inner, psychic 'object' in the infant.

conscious. Thus, the sigh in deep meditation does not mean a shattering lament, an abysmal pain, but rather something auratic that has not yet been fully achieved: death the 'other way round'.

This is also the view of Leikert, who further critically notes that classical psychoanalysis has increasingly solidified in the direction of a language-based, lexeme-oriented way of working. As Leikert notes, nowadays the only therapeutic approach is in the direction of a social reality and a rigid linguistic-external subject-object duality. The symbolic, the Speaks, is emphasized, but what is missing is the "engagement with the sensual logic of perception, especially with the rhythm of binary perception, with the "kinesthetic matrix of desire," writes Leikert.[34] What is meant is what the psychoanalyst H. Stein[35] also means by the psychoanalytic meditation and what the philosopher. D. Heller-Roazen[36] means with the "inner touch", the "inner sense", the constant tuning with one's own body image or self-perception in a more substantial form. Sometimes as a 'mountain', sometimes as a 'tree', sometimes as a point of lucidity or something else

---

[34] Leikert, S., Schönheit und Konflikt, Umrisse einer allgemeinen psychoanalytischen Ästhetik (Beauty and Conflict, Outlines of a General Psychoanalytic Aesthetics), Psychosozial Verlag (2012).

[35] Stein, H., Freud spiritually, Bonz (1997).

[36] Roazen, D., The inner sense, archaeology of a feeling, Fischer (2012)

consciously substantial like a life in dying, like a probatory death.

Psychoanalysis should not only be about the sober linguistic reference, but also about what art, religion and the "rhythmizing order of the ritual" contain. Instead of kinesthetics, we often speak of coenesthetics. Here the Rays are emphasized, but there is little access to the symbolic. Leikert states that there is a problem here, because the free associations and the equal suspended attention do not reach this level so well, and so they cannot be integrated enough into the subject through symbolic, through words.[37] For this purpose, an additional procedure is needed like the *Analytic Psychocatharsis*, which, however, has to establish a special access to the also clearly expressible truth in the already indicated pass-words, as I will further show.

So it is about an inner self-awareness, an immediate familiarity, a love to this something, what the psychoanalyst N. Symington calls the 'Thathood', the 'Dasheit', something similar to Roazens 'inner touch'. With this, people used to be able to communicate directly with each other. They communicated, so to speak, with their inner touches, from touch to touch, from 'skin to skin'. I could

---

[37] With kinesthetics is rather meant an inner movement, with coenesthetics more this "inner-touch" of D. Heller-Roazen. I use both in the same way. As I will explain, the Koine (Greek) is the common sense, the connecting feeling.

also say from body image to body image, from the inner 'mountain' of one to the inner 'mountain' of the other, to bring my example back into play. From love to death and from death to love, whereby people then knew the spun web of Lacanian 'jouissance' better than we do today. In this web one has to take the unconscious like a burden on oneself like Aeneas his father Anchises when he had to carry him on his back out of the burning Troy. Just as today we have to shoulder the father principle, the determiner logic, even Freud himself (albeit supplemented by 'visions').

The concept of the body-image, that is, of the body-image-acting, was propagated above all by the French psychoanalyst F. Dolto. It is about this kin- or coenaesthetic image-feeling that one has of one's own body within oneself. Even from the point of view of awareness, we do not perceive ourselves with the same concentration in all parts of our body. The ancient Greeks felt themselves most intensely in the diaphragm (phren). Others are head people or feel themselves mainly in the musculoskeletal system close to the self. But it is mainly about the unconscious feeling of the 'inner touch'. This is perceived when meditating or practicing the mentioned *Analytic Psychocatharsis*. During these exercises some people speak of a 'trickling through', tingling or being shuddered through. Some also experience a brightness, liberation (catharsis), and emphasized inner relaxation. In any case, it is a more elementary self-experience up to autochthonous enjoyment, to 'jouissance' in the body image.

F. Dolto distinguished the dynamic, erotic and basal body image. With this she comes again close to the image of the corps morcelée, only that she determines these three pieces from her clinical experience, where they are not completely fragmented. Psychoanalysis is predominantly concerned with the first two, because large parts of them are unconscious. Even more unconscious, however, is probably the basal body image, which could now again be connected with Leikert's kinesthetics and is precisely not covered by conventional psychoanalysis. It is exactly that which has to do with rhythmicity, oscillation, pulsation but also the metrics of patterns or first " determining images". The signifiers, "the natural symbols have emerged from a certain number of " determining images " - from the image of the human body, from the image of a number of clearly visible objects like the sun, the moon and some others. And this is what gives human language its weight, its driving force, and its emotional vibration."[38]

Here the pictorial and the verbal seem to be summed up, but this is not quite the case. Seen in this way, my 'mountain' is not only a phallic symbol, but something summa-

---

[38] Lacan, J., Seminar II, Walter (1980) p.388 The imaginary signifier first in the foreground is thus clearly separated / connected in relation to the symbolic signifier.

rizing all the body images named by Dolto, all the Rays. But it does not speak clearly enough. As I said, the 'mountain' moved and radiated in the sense of the dynamic body image, but it also rested on a firm foundation and could be held for a while like the 'tree' of my adept. It was basal and probably also a little dynamic and erotic body image. The summary of all the partial aspects gives to the whole this substantiality which I have already conjured up several times, which nevertheless still remains too much arrested in the imaginary-real and must be symbolized still further, must be interpreted significantly, in order to really get into the 'other way round' of the image-word-acting bundled to the unity.

After all, a certain consistency of soul, firmness, is reached with it, which, moreover, would be accessible to a rational interpretation. For how St. Mechthild interprets her 'flowing light' is not antirational. Her ratio, with which she accompanies her highly erotic prayers, namely by the reference to Jesus and the 'Holy Spirit' completely in the sense of the valid religious constitution of that time, is structurally composed in exactly the same way as Freud's libido as eroticized psychic energy, which, after all, also serves sublimation, refinement, spiritualization, mathematization.It can also desexualize itself as Freud said, and thus it can even lead to a desire for love, even if for Freud such a striving, such a subject state concerning love, consisted above all in the longing for the love of the father and his corresponding, equivalent reaction.

In this respect, Mechthild's desire for love was a kind of identification, a kind of 'holy self-mind,' not an object-love in which, for Freud, an object, a human being, becomes libidinously occupied. But the word father was not always ideal for this, which is why Freud brought into play the so-called 'father of the ancients,' that is, a special ancestral figure, a symbol of strong memory of the creator of a clan, a people, or more. But even such an 'old man with a beard', as I already christened him, remained shadowy, imprecise, which is why Lacan converted him to the 'father name', to the signifier of a general father-hood (here ostensibly the symbolic signifier is meant). But even this did not outlast everything.

Lacan had for a long time - obedient to Freud - paid homage to this concept of the father coming from early times, prehistoric times, and then from the Bible, because finally something was needed that could be contrasted with the powerful, fascinating female-maternal central figure that still rules in the unconscious even of modern people.[39] For a scientifically thinking psychoanalyst, this could not be a god, which represents an idealization and a concealment of power. But the paternal name, this chorus of paternal voices, the superego, the most eloquent of all headlines - all these power-language attributions were

---

[39] In former times it was mother deities, today it is the imago of the very early seducing, loving, but also witch-like aggressive mother in the unconscious.

one day no longer sufficient for Lacan to define what should constitute the father as a symbolic, word-worker.[40]

In his XIX Seminar, therefore, he made an about-face; he subjected the father to an 'other way round' and said that one could see "how I used to explore in various registers above all the father metaphor, the proper name. There was everything it took to make sense of this mythical elaboration of my saying with the Bible [regarding the Father's name]. However, I will never do that again, I will never do that again, because, after all, I can be content to formulate things on the level of the logical structure, which, after all, has its rights. Voilà!"[41] The structure of logic, admittedly, sounds more sophisticated and scientific than the patriarchy, which reminds one of old patrician dynasties or even of what was quite wrongly called patriarchy, because in reality it was andriarchy, male supremacy.

I have given this the name "logical self-structure" in another book, because the logical structure alone sounds again too much only like philosophy, like academic guild. It must be about a self-logic, a self-analysis, about a - if I can already anticipate the next chapter - love for oneself as a logician, as a scientist from the subject. If

---

[40] In the Greek tragedy, the chorus in the background conveyed this linguistically powerful patristic. Nowadays the definition of the father as the creator of the word, the language, the linguistic was also tried.

[41] Lacan, J., Seminaiere Nr. XIX, Ed. Seuil (2011) p. 104

instead of logic I have presented with the 'mountain' and the 'tree' something which instead of 'vision' might perhaps be called the 'iconic', this serves exactly the same purpose, namely to move away from the old metaphors and concepts even insofar as they still have validity in classical psychoanalysis.[42] I have conceded that the 'iconic', the image-acting structure, alone, however, is not the last of wisdom either. The body images brought to unity do not hold together eternally by themselves.

That is why they flow through the human being like light in Mechthild's visions, which reminds us of the 'flowing rhythm' that Lacan considered to be the female libido. While in the male the libido flows outward, in the female it closes into a circle. By moving, it follows the flow of the tides of her fertility and pregnancies, menstruation and the gift of the breast in the breastfeeding process, and many affects and feelings reminiscent of the 'flowing light'. It gives the woman an inner solidity to which the male envy now refers quite intensely (especially as a

---

[42] With the term 'iconic' or of the iconics I want to avoid what comes close to a pictorial science, if this would not be such a dry, little expressive method. Iconic turn, pictorial turn, imagic turn, visualistic turn, were constant attempts in the nineties to create science from the imaginary side. The spiritualized, refined image of the icon with the concept of the 'iconic' comes closer to what is at stake in the vision-like processes, if one wants to understand it outside any religious classification. It is also not about a cult status, but about psychoanalysis.

counterpart to the female 'penis envy' unhappily postulated by Freud).

Summarized: The image-acting, the Id Rays, the coenaesthetic of love, the 'imaginary-real, 'iconic' concerns the one side of soul forces. It needs the other side, the logical structure (word-acting, the Id Speaks, the rhetoric of death, the symbolic-real) to it, it needs both (iconic and logical) together to understand and treat the human soul also in its unconsciousness. The 'logical self-structure" now represents only a supplement to the body-image self-structure. I repeat that in the end only the individual himself can define it in and out of himself, what it is about here, because it also needs the 'other way round' of image and word, of love and death', and about this nothing more can be said at all.

I could also have written about the 'other way round' of 'man and woman, of 'politics and stupidity' or of 'beauty and evil'.It doesn't matter, because the essence consists in the 'other way round' of each of these couples, of which the one part, the love - I also repeat this again - has to do with the lucidity, the look, the Id Rays. Death, on the other hand, is the mentor of expressing oneself, which in man (if he does not use the fist) comes to speak in the speaking, in the Id Speaks. Only by the fact that both come together in the experience of the individual in the psychoanalytically underpinned, substantiated meditation, in the *Analytic Psychocatharsis*, and connect themselves most closely, the goal is reached. The goal of self-analysis, of the science of the subject, which as a science itself becomes an 'other way round', if only the individual as such counts in its realization and implementation.

The determining, refined, referring to images, the Rays, the imaginary signifier, is thus opposed by the symbolic signifier, the word-acting, the Id Speaks.[43] The 'vision' participates in both, even if the imaginary first captivates more. But light is faster than sound, and so the symbolic (the striking word 'mountain' or 'tree') comes only then. As for the real of the 'vision', it depends on the narrow, concretistic, the 'défiles signifiantes' (as Lacan calls these narrowings, tunnels from one to the Other, from the unconscious to the conscious and other psychic counter-occupations), which is to be the aim of the book and of the procedure of *Analytic Psychocatharsis*. A form of the 'défiles signifiantes' combined from the Id Rays / Speaks is found - but only purely f o r m a l l y in the formula words.

With them one can make a feast without much effort, a feast of awareness, because the monotony of the formula-words can lead to a narrowing and moderation of the blank, on the exterior directed waking consciousness. I describe it once as the experience to be one with oneself and the world, thus with what I have already called the

---

[43] In Lacanian nomenclature, this also corresponds exactly to the show and the speaking instinct.

One-sidedness. It is the experience that does not fully participate in the real, but has nevertheless approached it, and that demonstrates less awareness, but already more awareness, fulfilling. The formula-word does not promote what is understood by attention, which is merely a somewhat heightened consciousness. When Freud speaks of the therapist's 'equal-floating attention', this clearly aims more toward awareness, toward oneness with the patient. In order to let this become a celebration, however, further internalizations are needed instead of being focused on the external, more attentiveness instead of attention, more 'other way round' - also with regard to love and death - than adapted.

As promised I attach here briefly which meanings are hidden overlapping in the formula word E.N.S.C.I.S. N.O.M. So one can read - read clockwise - for example ENS, the being, CIS, this side, NOM, (abbreviation for) name, thus 'the being this side of the name'. But you can also start at the S and read SCIS NOMEN: you know the name. Going once from the C, one reads CIS NO MENS, this side I swim, O spirit. Starting from M at the top left, one reads MENS CIS NO, the thought this side, within No (from No). Going once from the C, one reads CIS NO, MENS, this side I swim, O spirit. starting from O, OMEN SCIS N, you know the omen N, and C IS NO-MEN S, a hundred this name S, etc. Actually, three different meanings are enough to ensure the disparity, the incompatibility of a common, closed sense of all meanings together. But as already emphasized, these 'défilés logiques', these narrowings of letters are worthless in content, they serve only the scientific plausibility.

St. Mechthild did not have and did not need such a plausibility, but for that she had to constantly "drink the water of torment and dwell in the true desert".[44] She also had to let God tell her sadisms, the usual 'défilés legiques' of women mystics. St. Theresa of Lisieux was much more brutal with herself, and Britta of Sweden also liked to imagine scenes of torture with which the beloved God would maltreat her. In the end, however, they achieved great awareness, even though they were unconscious of their desires.

---

[44] Mechthild von Magdeburg, The Flowing Light of the Godhead, Publishing House of World Religions (2010) I, 35

4. 'Iconic' and Female Discourse of Love

Again on love, of which to speak is still almost impossible; one should have a language without words, at least without whole sentences, Lacan explains in his twenty-first seminar. And elsewhere: "Love can only be understood in the perspective of demand. There is love only for a being which can speak, and which directs this claim specifically to being heard. Why? Well, heard because of something that could also be called well because of nothing. This does not mean that this reference of love to nothing will not bring one very far, because in this because of nothing exists already the place of desire. . . What is that which is desired? It is the desiring in the Other, which can only happen by classifying the subject itself as desirable."[45]

As already indicated above, there is no proof of love. Moreover, such a sentence as "I love you" sounds much too sweeping, too detached or even extortionate and is mostly aimed at the fact that one wants to be loved again and not stand alone in the world with it. The ancient Greek god Plutos (Πλοῦτος), wealth, is said to have said something like this to Penia (Πενία), poverty. The story was invented by Plato when he wrote how Penia

---

[45] Lacan, J., Seminar VIII, Die Übertragung (The Transference), Passagen Verlag (2001), S. 435

crouched at the steps of the palace until Plutos, drunk on nectar, came down and impregnated her (in modern and ironic terms, he left in a cigarette break from the feast but then devoted himself - quite socially conscious - to loving the poor. In another version, however, Penia is said to have made a pass at Plutos, she then gave birth to Eros, the god of love (and thus all divine powers were together again).

Just as the body images mentioned in the previous chapter all come together and lead to what I called an 'iconic'. It is a substantial 'iconic', because when the body images come together, overlap, they become perceptible, it possibly even comes to the mentioned 'trickling through', shuddering through. This happens sometimes by itself, thus also without external assistance as mentioned by the moving piece of music. More and more it becomes apparent that the 'iconic', the image-acting, imaginary-real has substance, enjoying substance. Freud had added it in the framework of the theory of substances to the 'extended substance' of Aristotle and the 'thinking substance' of R. Descartes as third in form of the sublimated libido, the 'enjoying substance'.

In this way love comes already once quite timidly into play. It is sublime, desexualized libido (also an expression of Freud) and thus also accessible to enjoyment in its autochthonous, independent form. Here one can feel the proximity to narcissism, to self-love, but also distinguish both from it. I remind you of the COO, the 'concret original object'. Even if it is an original construction, it does not apply only to one's own reflection, as was the case with the ancient youth Narcissus. Narcissus fell in love with his external image, with the pure reflection of a momentary gaze, but the 'iconic' of love is an outwardly radiating internal self-image, image-acting per se, which is permanent. Lacan spoke of the "ultrasubjective radiance," the far-glowing imaginary-real that cannot be seen externally, although in common parlance one speaks of the radiance of a personality.

Only a rogue recognizes a rogue and only a lover recognizes a lover and probably only an inner-image radiating a same one because both are inspired by an 'iconic' experience. This was also the motto of St. Mechthild of Magdeburg. Above all, she recognized that the 'iconic' of love is related to death. "Love should be mortal, immoderate, unceasing,"[46] she wrote. And so Mechthild's love was not endowed with Freud's desexualized libido, which is rather a contradiction, but rather with a violent libido, raw, ecstatic, and fully inflamed in the 'iconic,' as she further wrote in a poetry form:

He [the beloved] kisses her through with his divine mouth. Well with you, yes, more than well, because of the exalted hour!

---

[46] Mechthild von Magdeburg, The Flowing Light of the Godhead, Publishing House of World Religions (2010) I, 28

He loves her with all his might on the camp of minne
And she comes into the highest delight
And in the most intimate sorrow, she becomes rightly
aware of him.
Eia, love, now let yourself be minned.
And do not resist with dark senses. [47]

As already quoted, other mystics also used this iconic flaming discourse, and one wonders: how can love take on such proportions, does it overshoot the mark, for the sexual in the poem cannot be overlooked? Admittedly, there was no psychoanalysis at that time, but the misgivings of the aforementioned matron certainly had to do with the fact that Mechthild's texts seemed too ecstatic and to her. Only her confessor stood by her. The best way to understand the matter, of course, is to take the relationship of love to death into account.

In this sense Lacan claimed: "To love it takes three", the two lovers and death. In order to grasp what love is, it has always been described, sung about and painted in its relation to death. [48] The two of the lovers can only be understood against the background of the three (lovers and death). "What the Borromean knot illustrates for us is that the 2 arises only through the linking of the 1 with the 3,

---

[47] As above, II, 23
[48] Lacan, J., Seminar VIII, S. 160

Lacan therefore concludes.[49] This also follows conclusively from set theory, as well as from social and historical facts. The courtly love of the Middle Ages, for example, shows quite well how the troubadours had to lock up the women in golden cages, to make them feel, so to speak, at a distance from them. And all this only in order to be able to serve the king thus better as vassals; which means to risk death in battle. Without death no love, without love no death, normal or 'other way round'.

With the love to God it does not behave differently. Here, too, the believer swings himself up to great heights of feeling, but in order not to be able to escape death, but to get a substitute for it elsewhere. And today's psychoanalysts recommend right from the start to always consider the discrepancy of the eros-life and death instincts in love, because there is no way around it. This knowledge of the relationship between love and death must be experienced again and again. "The fact remains," Lacan wrote in addition to the above, "that love is the relation of the real to knowledge," and can only be found in this way.

"It makes its object out of what is missing in the real," he adds, which can only be understood starting from Freud. As mentioned, Freud called the balance of "ego libido and object libido" love. Now this already sounds very sober, academic and devoid of any feeling. Therefore

[49] Lacan, J., Seminar XXI, Lecture from 12. 3. 1974, Staferla free

Lacan makes the suggestion that a lack in the real must not only be filled by the symbolic/imaginary with sense gestures (see Bo-Knot), but also more substantially with something tangible, with something 'inner touch' and 'jouissance feminine', the female enjoyment. In this way, love gets the same kind of 'objectness' as my 'mountain': auratic, not quite openly clarified visible, cloudy physical, intersubjective chill-out. Tangible love that seems to defy death.

But it does so only when united with death in the 'other way round'. For as much as my 'mountain' is a love of the Other, of nothingness, of emptiness in meditation, for example, I have had to push this 'vision' back again, because in a too-much-of-this, though not physical death, spiritual death looms. These are not new insights, they are just formulated a bit differently. So love is - following Lacan - in the Bo-Knot itself, because it has really reached a form of the 'other way round', seen in this way. However, all this remains very, very, theoretical, topological and mathematical by Lacan.

So that love can get along with death, death must also have taken this 'other way round' form, namely to be a life while dying, which the banal death cannot catch up completely. In chapter 5 I will report in detail on this concept (life while dying), insofar as it concerns the real end of life, something from recent neuroscientific findings. But the same concept can be applied to *Analytic Psychocatharsis*, in that meditation into the darkness, into nothingness, before oneself is like dying, but leading to a special kind of life. This is not a secret either. In Zen Buddhism, subjects are guided to love their teacher and his Koan, an enigmatic word, turned toward total unknowability, impossibility, groundlessness. And yet - if they are lucky - this 'other way round' of love and death opens up for them, because they lose themselves completely in this mysteriousness, but experience themselves again as if reborn, as Otherness, as Other. But this is mysticism, on which I do not base myself, and thus can only use it allegorically.

To the further and perhaps also better understanding: the knowledge in the love has only each of the two lovers to the half. This is also connected with the fact that one can only half tell the truth - no matter whether with regard to love or elsewhere. In order to tell the truth completely and to be fully involved in love, one would have to grasp the other just as holistically and include him in the event, which the very great lovers in literature, art and general life design have tried again and again, even if they have probably never succeeded perfectly. Even Jesus, this great lover, at the end of his life and the loss of his love relationship exclaimed: "Eloi, Eloi, lema sabachtani! My God, my God, why have you forsaken me!"[50] He still loved and lived intimately while dying, and many

---

[50] Mk 15, 33, 34. One has also wanted to understand the text as a recitation of Psalm 22, 2. But even if it is so, one exclaims such a thing only if one feels the same as the psalmist.

claimed that he was not dead when they laid him in the grave. Did he not succeed in an 'other way round' of love and death?

In any case, the philosopher D. Precht (a modern German neophilosopher) has succeeded (ironically said). According to him, love is a normal improbability, but that is what makes it precious.[51] "When I care about my partner, I do it 'out of love.' I do things I would never do, out of love. I watch movies at the cinema that I would never watch alone, and listen spellbound to thoughts that would never interest me in other people." Finally, he thinks that nowadays - since all his descriptions of what love really is remained without results - one can only love as love itself, solipsistically so to speak. Precht's book of four hundred pages on biology, sociology and psychology of love is a good example of the popular scientific pathos. Only one sentence on psychoanalysis; it teaches, Precht says, that love arises from sexuality. The psychoanalytic talk shows the opposite: nothing is more threatening than sex (the question of orientation, frequency, quality, constant failure, etc.).Sex as already said is only the metaphor for a constant failure, an illusory relationship. The man always ejaculates at the climax of his anxiety, at the moment of not knowing any further, Lacan thinks.

---

[51] Precht, D., Liebe, ein unordentliches Gefühl (Love, A Messy Feeling), Verlag Goldmann (2009) especially pp. 284 - 287

Now I don't know if Lacan gets very much further in terms of more explanations of love. Even if he says that there is true love only to a name, in order to avoid that one could ascribe too great a value to the love of objects, he thereby remains in the narrow, the exclusive reference to the word-acting. This also underlies the love of transference, which is so important in psychoanalysis. As said, transference means that the patient transfers to the psychoanalyst in a positive or loving way feelings, fantasies, attitudes and above all symbolically conceived meanings. Since these are usually inadequate, the transference must be resolved therapeutically. Even if the word-acting has advantages, nothing of love remains. But why not let the image-acting, the 'iconic', come into play as well? For love, this would have even more advantages, especially in combination with the word.

In a lecture to prospective psychiatrists, which also deals with love, Lacan turns to his listeners almost in despair and confesses that he will not be understood.[52] Yes, one is not supposed to understand him completely, because the people who understand each other too well, who therefore love each other, are not the ones psychoanalysis is about. Rather, it is about those who misunderstand each other, husband and wife, for example, where words often fail. "Here," Lacan continues, "the function of the

---

[52] Lacan, J., An die Psychiater (To the Psychiatrists), RISS, Vortrag vom 10. 11. 1967

real comes into play. Thus love proves itself to be 'contingent' in its origin and at the same time proves the contingency of truth in relation to the real." This is to say that love consists of an inner necessity, but whom does it help to put it this way?

It was not only Lacan who found himself in the difficulty and despair of expressing it and not being able to understand it. Even my meditation teacher Kirpal Singh, who had many students in America, Europe, India and a few other countries, and for whom the subject of love was extremely important, could hardly convey anything thoughtful about it. Finally he said, take the meditation teacher himself, take me as the object of your love, because I love you too, but it was clear to him and to everyone else that this was also just a desperate call.

Because if he were to die, where would one be? One would be lost in this kind of love sickness, because death in its normal form is always present in such a sickness, and thus one can likewise only cry out: why have you left us? He himself had been like this at the death of his teacher, he told quite openly, and so he had to retire for a long time to the roughest parts of the Himalayas and meditate. Like St. Mechthild, he had to mortify himself in order to be able to be credible again. "Fasting, waking, scourging, confession, groaning, weeping, praying, and hard conquest of the senses," she demanded of herself, which was a bit too much, for she deserved a better life.[53] But one finds out of the entanglements of love and death only with their 'other way round', which she certainly succeeded in part, but so martial for today is no longer meaningful and comprehensible.

I knew some people whose training analyst died during the long training or whose therapeutic psychoanalyst died during the therapy. It was terrible, for these people it was as if they had once again lost their mother and father and all the others with whom they had a deep relationship. They wandered around as they did on the first day of their psychoanalytic relationship, or hid their dismay behind the most varied explanations, which showed quite clearly that they had become too dependent. They all got totally involved in love, and then they realized that it was, after all, a form of nothingness, of madness, of the cruelest seduction. They couldn't make anything else out of it that could have been understood.

So I'm no better off for it, I'll be just as little understood, and although I don't mind it much, the thing still drives me. For even my teachers and patrons have already died, and I sometimes berate them for not having brought me completely out of confusion. They gave me their wisdom, which ran through my life like a red thread, an Ariadne's

---

[53] Mechthild von Magdeburg, The Flowing Light of the Godhead, Publishing House of World Religions (2010) VII, 65

thread (Lacan would mean thread geometry). And now? The thread behaves like the baton in the relay race, which must not fall down, otherwise the fight is lost. One must continue to carry the baton, to continue to spin the thread, and once it has been woven and braided, one cannot stop. But how to continue?

External teaching material for this is abundant, but how can one be sure to have received the order to continue only from oneself? Does one have to love oneself in the 'iconic' and 'rhetorical', that is, in the form that the teachers have left to one, that is, find one's place the 'other way round'? I had a patient who, after a long inner search and with reason in his voice, said he was God. So he was not one of those who run around shouting 'I am Jesus, I am Jesus'! He was not psychotic, worked as a gardener, had social contacts, and I could observe his behavior for many years. He could love just like that, only in this divine way, but why not. He liked to argue with strict believers or clergy, quoting to them from the New Testament John 10:34: "Is it not written in your law 'I said you are gods'?"

Of course, he didn't get very far with that. In several of my books I have quoted the psychoanalyst. M. Mitscherlich, whose last book was entitled 'A Love of One' Self that Makes One Happy.' By this she probably meant the independence and detachment at work in her work with patients.[54] It was not a narcissistic love which is a pure, smooth specular reflection. It would have been better if she had written of a love for oneself as Other, because it is not narcissism or something egomaniacal. But basically it was once again about another attempt to say something authentically real about love. Because of course it is about something in oneself, but how does one get there in a form worthy of love?

Lacan made no secret of the fact that he did not appreciate the typical 'female love discourse'. Recently, the well-known actress Senta Berger was interviewed about the topic of love, and indeed, she started from her love for her mother, which still exists long after her death, and followed it up with some statements about her experiences of love, so what do you say about it. The philosopher and semiotician R. Barthes also tried to say more about it in his book 'Fragments of a Language of Love'.[55] He also held it with the figure of the Other to be written large, because significant, who, as said, with Lacan has to do with the father metaphor, but with Mitscherlich, Berger and Barthes with the premotherly.

---

[54] Mitscherlich, M., Eine Liebe zu sich selbst, die glücklich macht('A Love of One' Self that Makes One Happy), S. Fischer (2013)

[55] Barthes, R., Fragmente einer Sprache der Liebe ('Fragments of a Language of Love'), Suhrkamp (2015)

It is true that Barthes took over this being of the Other acting in and outside of him from Lacan, and it kept him from getting completely lost in the ups and downs of his - homoerotically marked - love. Barthes emphasizes having a feminine discourse, but he is feminized - he writes - as a man not because he is inverted, that is, homosexual, but because he loves. He loves and always wants to remain addicted to love as such, that is, that which is determined by the Other, despite all disappointments, crushes, jealousies, 'love sighs,' feelings of happiness and contrition.

"The linguistic staging [as the writer of his book] keeps the death of the Other at bay," Barthes explains, insisting on the affirmation, on the stubborn adherence to love, on the systematicity of love, which he also considers an almost "religious intimacy" that one could not avoid. Even if love is only "a swarm of figures," it is for him also the guarantor of a truth: "I let the Other exist in his truth," he argues further, which is no longer entirely credible, as I will describe. Barthes also quotes Goethe's Werther, who, regarding his love for Lotte, a married woman, fervently proclaims to his friend Wilhelm in a letter, "I sometimes do not understand how anyone else can love her, may love her, since I love her so completely alone, so intimately, so fully, know nothing else, nor know, nor have anything else than her." Well, that sounds a lot like narcissism and delusional misjudgment.

"Wilhelm," Werther also says to his friend in another passage that Barthes does not quote, but which demonstrates even more rigorously the ecstasy of this love, "what is the world to our hearts without love . . And how worthy I become of myself, how I - to you I may say it, you have a sense of such things - how I adore myself by her loving me!" But she does not love him, this narcissist, equally, if at all, and so he falls into a pronounced self-love by not even having such an Other as Barthes, who continues to write conclusively of himself, "In reality, conversely, the Other grounds me: only with the Other do I feel myself to be 'myself.' On the basis of this relationship, I know more about myself than all those who also do not know about me: that I love." And so his whole book becomes a comprehensive evocation of love. Did he have to defend it against his homosexual tendencies? Doesn't he himself sound a bit like the Werther he quotes? A bit narcissistic and over-romantic.

Yes, he had to defend himself, and not only because at that time homosexuality was not yet as tolerated, socially and administratively fully equal and accepted as it is today. Maybe he is not the narcissist himself, but he presents his love as the total mirror, in which first of all he himself is already to be seen in it, even if he means in the form of the Other. But is it not the same, the homo? Finally, he also went a step further, as it was also done by A. Gide, J. Genet and as recently known also by M. Foucault in the direction of pedophilia. He signed with many other intellectuals in the seventies of the last century an appeal for decriminalization of pedophilia, which is difficult to understand today, since so many cases of abuse with clear consequential damage to children and adolescents have become known.

I have tried to give a more intensive account of Barthes' biography. He lived most of his life with his mother, probably had many love partners, what he called his second family. For a long time he was ill with tuberculosis. The biographer H. Algalarrondo gives a negative picture of Barthes, writing that Barthes also frequented children's brothels and that his work was unspecial. He was perhaps a somewhat overblown shining light of the sixties, when people were finally beginning to be free, long young, gay or otherwise diverse and revolutionary. Today, people don't really appreciate the freedoms anymore. Recently (March 2021), the gay community and with it many others have strongly criticized that the Pope does not want to bless gay marriage.

It would be an act of love after all, and so some priests have already started blessing gay marriage. Why not, but don't the church and gays have to resolve an internal contradiction? If whistleblowers were to be awarded the Federal Cross of Merit, that might well be fair, but wouldn't the state and its secret-keepers first have to change the entire foundations of politics and appoint a mediator who would clarify with both parties the question of what data the people need, who is what and why for whom?

Does the church bless the homosexuals perhaps, because otherwise the customers run away from it? Or are the homosexuals looking for the seal of quality of a rumor society, which holds out the prospect of life after death to them? And how will it go on if the priests then also have to bless the fetishists, the voyeurs and the sadomasochists? In the blessing, as in the state secret, something paranoid is at play, a half-concealed discourse along the lines of "I see something you don't see," although both are blind. In my view, every sexuality has its shadow side that can be badly blessed, just as every person has secrets that should not necessarily be snitched on.

Also the heterosexual man, who constantly needs another woman and has ten more in his head, does not deserve a blessing for this - quasi perverted - inclination, if there is one at all. As much as marriage has a high status, a political value, a strong social orientation, it would never have occurred to me myself, for example, that priests could help me arrange my marriage. We live in the age of self-determination, in which one can borrow a bit from psychoanalysis, but will have to struggle decisively through efforts to achieve consensus among the partners. The man will not want to see the woman as a mother, the woman will not want to see herself as a sexual object, as all this is well clarified in the Oedipus complex structure. The homosexuals are usually well informed about the fact that they have a mother fixation and fear of the father's love, which I have often noticed in treatments as well. But in this discourse, in this psychoanalytic way of thinking, they do not want to enter. Yes, well.

I have commented on the transgender problem else-where,[56] here only briefly the following: the transgender does not want to be the other sexually determined gender, he only wants to be sexually the 'other way round' normal and recognized in this normality, because he does not get this recognition in the primary identity. Nevertheless, the genetic and especially the COO-determined gender iden-tity is an amorous obstacle. Young Werther's love for his Lotte may have been more of an amorous delusion that could have had such a delirious basis, as some transgender desires do. And so also the pope's blessing is to confirm that those joined in homosexual marriage are then n o r m a l gay!

So love and death cannot be understood the 'other way round'. This is how it behaves 'normally the way around'. Lotte was so sacred to Werther, Goethe wrote, that all desire fell completely silent in her presence. It was a completely sterile, sacralized and cultic love, but it was also 'normal around'. Werther did not have a complete Other; his friend Wilhelm clearly takes his place, he is a good friend, and Werther's letters to him fill almost the entire novel. But his and Barthes's Other was not com-

---

[56] Hummel, G., v., Overwhelmed, BoD, 2021

plete either, he was too attached to the female 'love discourse', of speaking in terms of an 'I love, therefore I am'. It is a speaking with which one wants to get out of speaking, and there love is supposed to be the decisive pivot.

Also the early Freud had in his colleague and mainly also pen friend W. Fliess a partner to whom Freud described all his thoughts especially concerning his neuro-psychological theories. It has always been said that Fliess was Freud's psychoanalyst to whom he could communicate everything and who participated in his development in an interpretive way. Freud himself wrote that Fliess was " . . the only Other, the alter per se," had been. At least this was the case in the very earliest period of the emergence of psychoanalysis.[57] Later, disputes arose, and so this Other also remained incomplete. The love of friendship between Freud and Fliess was not sufficient as a pivot.

The speaking of man - according to Lacan - began with the repetition of words of solution or identity. It still had quite a command and emphasis character, which is why one can assume a kind of 'empty repetition'.[58] As is well known, neurosis, also that of the conformists, the normality addicts, is dominated by a repetition compulsion, at least a repetition event, which arises with the first identity

---

[57] Gay P: Freud. Eine Biographie für unsere Zeit (A Biography for the Times now). Frankfurt a. M: Fischer 1995.
[58] Lacan, J., Seminaire XIX, Lecture from 4. 5. 1972

formations, about which I will still report in chapter 7. Something so intimately repetitive can also be inherent in a love stammer, as one often has the impression with Barthes. In his case, of course, it is not the usual talk, the social gossip, which is also often 'empty repetition'. But even love thoughts can seem like that, if they are constantly delivered with the same artful warmth.

Barthes just took the standpoint: "Better the mirages of subjectivity than the fraud of objectivity. Better the imaginary of the subject than its censorship." The 'iconic' of my 'mountain' imaginary-real, however, I certainly want to subject to censorship. It is to be a feminine discourse, but one that at the same time takes into account the activity of the signifier, that is, one that also takes into account the linguistic-symbolic and thus has a claim to a 'logical praxis,' to a science of the subject and thus to a complete discourse that includes the Other as effectively Other.

My 'mountain' is only an occupational therapy with the image-acting, but one which leads me beyond it into the catharsis, into the 'trickling through', which can bring me at all to come to the original word-acting of the password. Only in this way it is possible to penetrate the - against the background of the existing - nothing, and to utilize the death that connects the two. "Thou shalt minne the Nothing und shalt fly the Egoisting", Mechthild expresses this fact poetically. One must love the nothing, must 'minnen' it properly, that is an act of death, with which the 'other way round' of love and death is realized. I have to take down from my 'mountain', my 'tree', all the meanings that still harbor egomaniacal and only have to transfer its lucidity into the symbolic, which in Lacan's knot is filled with death. But what do I do with it then? Well, I orient myself to the pass-words.

One can understand this - as already indicated several times - also in this way: The speaking, the communication never works one hundred percent. People constantly talk past each other, no speech, no matter how sophisticated, is immune to misunderstandings. Even the best legalese is counter-communicative, because one can hardly follow the multiple nested sentences used there. That is why psychoanalysts came up with the idea to look for the truth especially in lies. Since the patient is supposed to 'free-associate', he sometimes can't lie so perfectly, and so one can get on his nerves. The usual speaking, the normally symbolic, has rightly been placed by Lacan in the loop marked by the word death.

In order to come into connection with the real, the analytical discourse must therefore disregard the too superficial sense and invoke to be able to recognize either the JΦ, the plaisir phallique, the male-dominated, phallic enjoyment behind everything said and thus unmask the truth. Or he must work out what the JA, the 'jouissance de l'Autre', the enjoyment of the Other, the feminine enjoyment might signify. The oral, the anal, the phallic, the gaze and the voice as psychic objects are the bases of conventional psychoanalysis; everything is worked through with them, but this is not a final solution. Everything is based on the fact that until today no clear statement for the relation of the sexes has been found. Even Lacan, so shrewd in this sector, thought that woman could only be happy in a state of a kind of nationalization. Jesus!

Several times Lacan described the relation man/woman in a mathematically complex quantifier logic, which is intellectually brilliant. However, even if it is understood as a psychoanalytic theory, it can only be applied with difficulty by the professional in the therapeutic session. For a philosophical, sociological and other use one has to translate it into a more easily understandable concept, which I will try to do here: Lacan assumes that the man, the speech and the sexual function as a trinity produce a real initial situation which puts the phallic enjoyment (the phallic signifier) in the center. It is this three that makes the beginning, which Lacan also underpins with set theory, where the three is the least one starts with.

The man can't say no to the phallic enjoyment (plaisir phallique) in principle because of this dominating three, he remains 'finite' in it, number-conform, but he counts only himself, while the woman has the possibility of saying no to it. But what does she gain from using this possibility? She remains like the virgin in the area of the not countable ones, of the always same ones and needs so something continuing. The situation is - as one says mathematically - undecidable, and so in this conflict the father-principle, father as ONE, as universal metaphor, gets the decidability, with which he/she raises the woman into the circle of the male and female determiners , whereby she becomes countable. Countable, she is entitled to everything, the freedom to determine, but also to have 'visions'.

So she doesn't need to be nationalized, because even if women were in the majority in this hypothetical state that nationalizes people, they wouldn't agree with such a notion of state incorporation and thus probably subordination. They don't need any paper at all, on which something regulating, giving a frame for their being or any other XY is written (I take these signs, because they already represent the male in the chromosome set). While the man brings himself only as "any" into the position of the conjugal or also not conjugal relationship, because he is 'finite' and counts only his equals, the woman becomes 'countable' with regard to the mathematically logical father principle, and is existent especially in relation to herself as "every woman".[59] The wisdom last conclusion is perhaps also not yet.

But asked differently, if it is true that the woman takes the reference to "every woman", to the all of the feminine, in the general society, to be a woman, why should all - and of course not only the women - still spend hundreds of hours in psychoanalysis? Because there, first of

---

[59] Lacan, J., Seminaire XVIII, Edit. Seuil (2006) S. 147

all, one would not need any concept, framework, state or number-theoretical at all, and how would one call the result? With the speaking, the word-acting alone, which is male-dominated (master discourse, signifier 1) it would not succeed, after all. Again I am at the point where one has to ask about the union with the 'iconic', the one dominated by the feminine, and where I can offer my *Analytic Psychocatharsis*, in which after the entry into the image-acting, 'iconic', the leap into the word-acting is made possible precisely because here it is no longer the plaisir phallique, but the 'jouissance' as such, the catharsis, that governs the situation.

I remind again of Freud's hypnoses, which could not correctly verify what was heard and said, but the word-acting was used. Lacan, of course, did not mean it as blatantly as formulated above: In order not to subordinate women to the father metaphor alone, the psychoanalysts looked for a special, female logic, self-logic. But the word logic is also poorly suited for a distinction into male and female, when - in the unconscious - man and woman are the same. That is, until all eternity one will say male and female, man and woman, X and Y, whereby in each case other conditions, other words and other pictures, will be responsible for it. Here I propose to find a successful, matured, good combination of the two in the form of the Rays / Speaks by the application of the *Analytic Psychocatharsis*.

For such an element of solid fusion has been lacking up to now. With the philosophers it lacks the practice, with the many psycho-practices which are offered today it lacks clear, scientifically precise theory and with the psychoanalysts often still this successful, matured, good combination of the basic forces in the practice is missing, which comes above all by the undervaluation of the image-acting one by imputing to him that he is after her. She lets the father-principle merge into the total Minne, which thus represents the perfect ONE. But with all the counter-principles (devils) and for lack of scientific theory, she has to suffer terrible agonies and even inflict some on herself. However, she uses a clever psychoanalytical trick in order not to appear too suggestive.

As is well known, the psychoanalyst has to impose the so-called basic rule on his patient, namely to say everything that always comes to mind, even embarrassing and stupid things. The imposition of the basic rule is basically a manipulation that disturbs the free, associative encounter between analyst and patient from the very beginning. Only, how should he do it differently? A. Ferro said, "with the basic rule you are already putting one on a preset road", that is no longer spontaneous.[60] He tries "tell something", but this is often the most disturbing. Just tell? Yes what? Similarly, Mechthild arranges this with

---

[60] Ferro, A., Pensieri di uno psicoanalista irriverente (Thoughts of an irreverent psychoanalyst), Raffaelo Cortina (2017) p. 64

her God by implying that he is after her. For with her, both are eager to tell.

She first assigned the Father or ONE principle to God and that means to the Minne as such, the divine Minne. Freud would say, this is the utmost what one can achieve with a self-sublimation. But Mechthild achieves even more. It is not she who is minne-sick, "he [God] is minne-sick after her," she argues.[61] He is after her, wanting to minne her wherever and whenever possible. This is clever, if a bit unsettling, but is a stable starting position, and so she can establish her doctrine and write of her experiences. Few recognized her at the time.

Nevertheless, one can assume that she was happy. Although a stranger and alone, having come to Magdeburg at the age of about twenty, she had joined a lay order as a Beguine. She gained listeners and readers, was also asked for advice on general questions of life, and only withdrew to a monastery for the last twelve years of her life. She had vision-like experiences already as a teenager, and throughout her life she needed no one else, for she had simply chosen the Most High as her Beloved, and what could go wrong? Even if one disregards the super-spiritual and unconsciously eroticized, one must call her a great personality from whom one can still learn a lot until today.

---

[61] Mechthild von Magdeburg, The Flowing Light of the Godhead, Publishing House of World Religions (2010) II, 2

5. Death, the absolute Master?

I have now devoted three chapters predominantly to the theme of love, now it is death's turn, for it is just as necessary for the ultimate Oneness, both in Lacan and in Mechthild. The Oneness could look like the ONE Lacan aimed at in his Bo-Knot, but can best be represented by addressing love in its relation to death from the latter's side much more directly. This is, of course, an ancient undertaking; it already occurs in Orpheus and Eurydice, where love conquers death but then fails. Or with Sisyphus, who even twice outwits death (Tartarus), about which I have reported elsewhere. Furthermore, there has always been a dispute about whether there is life after death or rather not. But newer neuroscientific investigations could solve this dispute in a way that does justice to both views and still has a bit to do with love. One more thing.

In this regard, I am talking about life i m dying or even life i m death, i.e., a state that is seen from the outside as the end of life and can be precisely determined with electroencephalography, functional magnetic resonance technology and other scientific methods. But from the inside this death looks completely different.This is not only claimed by many mystics or myth tellers, I will also quote neuroscientists and give psychoanalytical arguments how in the transition from life to a very last death still other, such regressive, i.e. returning to more elementary psychic constitutions, involutive processes have meaning in the dying process.[62] Because said so, dying can not only be learned, as one can often hear from esotericists, but can be experienced in its psychic structure long before, for which just a connection of love and death of a completely different kind is necessary.

In Holy Week 2019, the neuroscientist Nedan Sestan published an article in the renowned journal Nature in which he described how brain cells in animals still gave neurological signs of life hours after their death and thus without oxygen. The researchers clarified that the brain was no longer supplied with blood, but that the vascular system was only filled with an inert, i.e. non-reactive, stagnant fluid. "The researchers were able to show on tissue samples of brain that its neurons exchanged electrical signals after appropriate stimulation. The death of brain cells after a lack of oxygen was apparently a gradual process."[63] So there is not only a brain metabolism, but there is an information exchange in the neuronal network of the brain. Of course, this has nothing to do with

---

[62] I understand this exactly as a counterpart to the evolution which has lasted hundreds of millions of years. But this does not contradict the fact that a retrograde process in an elementary genetic process is possible in a short time.

[63] Albrecht, J., Brendler, M., Bericht (Report) in the FAS vom 21. 4. 2019. p. 53

the concept of life as we usually use it for our existence.[64] But something is still there and deserves the term life, even if in a completely different way.

This can be seen just by how and what was further stated in the discussion about this neuroscientific study by N. Sestan in Nature. On the one hand, that these neuron signals could be detected up to six hours after the death of the animal and thus without oxygen supply. On the other hand it was argued that in this time after the official death determined from the outside despite the continuing reaction signs with no kind of reanimation again real life, thus brain activity with "higher functions" could be expected. Life would thus be terminated anyway and thus the study would not be very interesting, one of the study commentators claimed. But what does terminated really mean here and what, moreover, does "higher brain functions" mean? Is it even a matter of such specifics?

As mentioned by the terms regression, mental return, or even involution to early childhood stages of experience, such states are known in psychology and neurology, and especially in psychoanalysis, as necessary and much more important for certain recovery and restoration processes than the fully conscious, spiritually higher state.

---

[64] There has always been talk of different stages of death, but scientific proof is worth more than myth.

One does not speak then of 'deeper brain functions' but of more elementary, primordial brain functions or - as Freud did - of the primordial repressed, i.e. the first repression, a state of psychic necessity with which then the less repressed areas can be explained. This state is also common to the events in the realm of the representation of the imagination and the earliest drive linkages (Id Rays / Speaks).My 'mountain' is only a 'shift' of this drive linkage into the 'iconic', that is, it emphasizes particularly strongly the pictorial side of this very early mental construction.

Just these more elementary states - whether one understands them neuroscientifically or psychoanalytically is irrelevant - are significant and important for life in the original sense, in the unconsciously psychological and in the physically biological. Especially the neurologist A. R. Lurija established a connection between brain and unconscious decades ago, relating the Freudian 'id', i.e. the reservoir of the driving forces with midbrain and diencephalon regions. So it is not about the cerebrum and its so-called "higher brain functions", which are essential for the basis of the soul, but just about the more elementary levels and functions, which are not inferior soul-wise. On the contrary, in the love life and in dying they even take the main position.

The ego (including ego ideal and superego, the planning and all-thinking frontal brain, as well as the isolated word and image processing (in the temporal and in the posteri-

or lobe) only disturb the basic soul, which comes into play in dreams, but also in meditation, in certain religious experiences, in psychoanalysis and above all in the dying process. This aspect of a somehow life while dying, which I would prefer to call even the life i n death (as opposed to one after death), is important for the debate about an 'other way round' (of love and death). For a possible reanimation and return to so-called 'higher brain functions' (with which, moreover, often the most terrible things are done), this kind of life thus no longer plays such an important role. This is also not necessary, perhaps even a prerequisite for this life of a completely different kind to still take place.

For the life in the regression (or mental-physical involution) grasped from the psychoanalysis, this still for hours lasting phase of neuro-psychic processes, as Sestan has explored it, is a real 'other way round'. In the vernacular it has always been said that in the last moments of leaving, drifting away, the whole life runs again in front of you like in a movie. But I don't believe that it behaves like that and it doesn't bring anything, because it doesn't convey a solution. Rather, it seems credible what relatives of my patients often told me, that the facial features of the deceased had changed long after the so-called time of death. In most cases they would have taken on more relaxed or other characteristic forms. So the dying person still experienced a special facial expression.

Between the life with "higher brain functions" and the final death there is thus obviously an extended intermediate realm. So one could also say that one does not have to outwit death like Sisyphus, but life, even in death (or at least in dying) still to outlast something. For what we need is a subject 'without a head,' as Lacan says, that is, without headiness, as represented by the "higher brain performances.[65] The unconscious knowledge of truth pushes outward, but directly (from the irrational to the rational as in the psychoanalytic session) the unconscious can no longer perform such a consciousness in the dying state; it is, after all, in the aforementioned naive awareness in which one no longer needs sophisticated logical interpretations.

The awareness, this mental 'other way round', is also found in the intermediate realm of dying, and it exactly resembles the awareness of the early hominids, concerning which I have already reported S. Klein's thesis of the most primal creativity. Sestan is right, one does not need much brain for it, the third which the hominids had is enough. But for this, the soul in this .state finds the perfect entanglement of inside and outside, i.e. it does not take this difference for important anymore and still creates the most essential combinations of these two basic elements of the psychic, which I call the image- and the

---

[65] Lacan, J., Seminaire XI, Seuil (1964) S. 165

word-acting (Lacan's imaginary and symbolic signifiers), in itself.

That is, in this state of the intermediate realm there is only a very reduced consciousness, but all the more awareness, of which I have already reported.[66] Awareness is the simpler, more direct way of attention, a kind of clairaudience and clairvoyance reminiscent of the lucid dream, and it is most concentrated, most penetrating and most pointed in the most regressive, already half-dead state. When one says of someone that he lives consciously, one does not mean that he is awake conscious, that he has mirror consciousness, but that he is interwoven with a purposefulness or clarity orientation that goes only inward. It is about an exclusively into the deepest (or highest) directed not perception of truth but perception of reality, primary imagination, fusion of Eros and death, awareness per se.

This is also the reason why I have spoken about the steps by which one can learn to die even before the very last death, that is, already having made similar experiences with regression, mental withdrawal and processing of primary psychic structures. Because it is probably possi-

---

[66] I will refer later to the consciousness researcher G. Tononi, who attributes consciousness even to lowest existences. Awareness can reach only the human being.

ble through an intensive meditative, psychoanalytical, a somehow renewed self-sublimating training or something else similar, to establish, to 'visualize' or to imitate a dying in life, that is to structure it as authentically as possible, in order to benefit from it for the actual life. For only in this way does it make sense to answer anew the question about life i n death, as it was taken up, among other things, by the article in the journal Nature.

Rather a look into the fusion longing or the corresponding phantasm, which probably has to do in connection with the separation from the mother and even more - as mentioned - from the placental co-consciousness, or arises in the early trauma, helps. A real fusion is never satisfied or sufficiently achieved in ordinary life. In the phase of this life while dying, however, it obviously becomes possible, rudimentarily experienced or regressively/progressively completed. All this explains why in the religious sphere and elsewhere there is talk of a life after death.

One cannot imagine namely that the life should be terminated without a meaningful and redeeming process. But that after a total bodily disintegration somewhere else entirely, some kind of life is possible again, sounds implausible. And so, from the point of view of psychoanalysis as well as from the point of view of religious, spiritual understanding, there is a plausible solution to the problem if one concentrates on this special phase of an awareness in the dying process, an awareness of existence in its 'other way round', instead of making delusional hopes.

The Tibetan Book of the Dead is also about this intermediate realm, but here it is about the time between death and the rebirth that comes about at the end of life.[67] And this life while dying, which does not have to be a transmigration of souls at all, but is a static process, is about the love for certain gods and not about one among humans.The dark, infrasonic sounds and chants are supposed to guide the dying person, who is hardly capable of hearing in the usual way, to cross something transforming, merging. Whether this can still work if one has not meditated before is probably questionable. But no matter, these are all only myths and mystical descriptions.

In the concept I want to present here, in a more differentiated way than I have cited in M. Mitscherlich, it is about the love for oneself, for oneself in the form of this Other, which had not been sufficiently pronounced in Werther through his friend Wilhelm and had remained somewhat frail and imprecise in Barthes. This Other is not imagined, imaginary, as Barthes sufficiently describes it for him, but it also participates in the other categories of Lacan's knot, in the symbolic and the real. And love to him and back from him is part of every psychoanalysis, even if it works there detached from sexuality, but not detached from libido. Even the aggression and the death

---

[67] Hauf, M., Das Tibetanische Totenbuch, Piper (2003)

is libidinous there, and so should enter into the aware-ness.

Whether the first Other is the mother or not does not mat-ter much. For the very early mother can be everything and nothing, the infant believes itself to be part of her, and then experiences her again as something monstrously Other, primordially repressed, of which nothing at all can be said, for words do not yet exist in this early phase. In psychoanalysis, we speak in this regard of the 'preoedi-pal', i.e. a somewhat unclear, immature and uncontrolled state of the soul, which is still before the one caused by the Oedipus constellation. In the Oedipus saga this is represented by the figure of the Sphinx. It is about the seducing but also aggressive mother Imago.

Also the concept of the 'identification with the aggressor' stated by A. Freud still seems to me as the most plausi-ble, because in the total helplessness towards an aggres-sor one is only screaming, aggressive against oneself and others. I don't remember anything like that, but a 'vision' and other constructions suggested something like that to me. So I once thought I had a trauma-related vision that depicted the war events in Finland when I was born, a kind of reincarnation phantasm (I died in Finland in the war events, so to speak, and was reborn somewhere else). But it was probably a Freudian screen memory. But what does this memory cover up? It must be the kind of memory that preserves what really took place without revealing it. The order of the imaginary-real is rather chaotic, but very soon I realized that the Finnish, white-clad soldiers are perhaps identical with the equally white-clad doctors, who already in my first year of life had been hard on me.

Because at that time there was an operation that did not go well. I had contracted an inguinal hernia. At that time, anesthesia was still simple. Intubation did not exist yet, direct oxygen-ether or oxygen-chloroform anesthesia was used. However, the doctors did not only operate on the hernia, but also took out my appendix at the same time, which probably served more for training purposes, because it was not inflamed. But this made the anesthesia too long and too uncontrolled. I suffered a severe transit syndrome, was no longer really there, banged my head back and forth for days and my feet together at the heels, so that deep wounds formed there, the scars of which could still be seen fifty years later.

It was something like Freud's first trauma, which is 'primal repressed'. As a later trauma, Freud describes the so-called traumatic 'primal scene' as the look into the parental bedroom. It is a scene of seduction, dramatic, erotic-aggressive, from which one is excluded, alien, outcast, as if betrayed and left alone, but this becomes traumatic only 'afterwards' - when one recognizes the connections. But my traumatic, anesthetic 'primal scene' was more painful, raping, physically hurting and confusing. In the bedside 'primal scene' the libidinous affect becomes repressed and traumatic in the embarrassment of the 'after the fact'. In the real trauma, however, a psychic part is largely split off. Even the mother can become the 'aggressor' if she does not adequately fulfill the child's wishes and the child is prematurely weaned from the breast or something else really hurtful happens.

The thing with Finland was an occultistic attempt of interpretation, an 'identification with the aggressor', an escape from the other and yet towards him. At that time I did not know that the Other has a double face and that one has to accept his negativity. Such a surgery and anesthesia trauma may well have provided the basis for a traumatic split. The strange memories now try to cover this up, and yet dealing with it was an experience that later enriched my life, for it led me to psychoanalysis and to writing about the process of *Analytic Psychocatharsis*.So no matter what the 'primal scene' or trauma looks like, one will never fully recall it, because this would only be hurting traumatic horror again or lead into neurosis, unless one learns l'Autre, that, to love the Other(s), also as death 'other-ways'.

One cannot experience death as such, as an absolute end, even if one has guessed it before. It can be circumscribed, but in the process it becomes more and more a something that one can deal with, even if it has negative sides. If people often think they have not been loved enough, it is always related to the fact that they have not understood that even, actively, even something like the negativity or the deadliness of the other, being able to love is worth more than anything else. Mechthild of Magdeburg knew this better than we do today, because she also had a concept for the deadly, for the 'other way round of love and death'.

"I like to die of love", she writes, with which she can ideally master the 'other way round of love and death'.[68] For she makes death her passion, but not because she is suicidal, but because it allows her to rise further in the enjoyment of her love. She knows that in the 'other way round' of love involved in dying, she will not really die at all, for "the clear love of playing tide prepares sweet distress for the soul, it kills it even without death."[69] To die the last death, or even to bring it about oneself, would be absurd, she says quite clearly. But one should be able to die also without the real death, one should learn it in time. One will learn it only by a cooperation of the 'other way round' of love, which will make the dying process, the deep regression into the unconscious, to a sweet misery. To a merging.

What Mechthild conveys so well is the combination of the two basic forces (similar to fusion), even if they admittedly do not convey the successful and fully matured kind. But the close connection of the forces is there, the alloying of the drives, as Freud says. This alloy, to be

---

[68] Mechthild von Magdeburg, The Flowing Light of the Godhead, Publishing House of World Religions (2010) II, 4

[69] Like above, II,13

sure, does not find full maturity or goodness even in the usually adapted human being, but becomes entangled in changing, psychic 'objects' (the oral, phallic, vocal, etc.). The goal in psychoanalysis is considered to be the 'good, constant 'object', the 'object constancy' of the matured psyche, which many psychoanalysts themselves fail to achieve. In Mechthild, at least, the 'object constancy' is always there, consisting in minne and simultaneous cognition. ("Minne without cognition methinks the wise soul darkness", she says).[70] Under it she would not do it.

Her love is not one of memory, just as her dying is forward, while most people die back into unconsciousness and unawareness long before the final end. It is good that they enjoy the life, the today's prosperity with house, garden, car, long-distance journeys and in the evening in nice restaurants meet friends to good meals . But then they accept the death that takes everything away from them and have never learned that one must die forward, not backward. Forwards, admittedly not into the finished picture, as theologians prophesy to them, but forwards into the dark, into the unknown, into the still undiscovered areas of the lower central nervous system or into the network of the unconscious, for communication with the other, into naive awareness (Mechthild already has all this behind her, since her dark is always illuminated).

---

[70] Like above, I, 21

In my youth, the Other was mostly still the father, with us in Germany even the Nazi father, and one internalized him together with his negativity. But as mentioned, for Lacan the father was no longer the standard, but the - equally internalized - the logical self-structure. The inner negativity, the thoughts one does not like or even hates in oneself, the negativity of the Other in oneself, rolls up the self-structure from the other side, from the 'other way round'. When it was said in the New Testament "Love your enemies", this sounds even more paradoxical than the call to love the negativity of the Other. But it probably means the same thing.

It concerns the same way, namely, to arrive at the same result via the construction of the 'iconic', via the image-acting built up into the fully human, via the Rays of a contradictory love, as philosophers have always done and psychoanalysts are now doing: to formulate a dialectic that begins with the thesis (e.g. to say that love is the basis of all being) which leads to the antithesis (that one gets nothing for it, for this passive love), which suggests the synthesis (namely to love the impossible, the seemingly hostile, the always encouraging to persevere, to endure nevertheless the negativity of the Other,

You have to love the Formula Words, that Lacanian braid that helps you pull yourself out of the psychic quagmire. What is pure fiction in Baron Munchausen is considered in *Analytic Psychocatharsis* as the part of a real ladder. Besides of love in the mentioned form, the form of the 'iconic', the image-true, the rays, it is now also death, the word-true, the speaking, the 'Cà parle dans l'inconscient', which has to be heard. Because, as I said, people usually speak past each other, but death speaks the truth. He says it because he is always the empty, the nihilating signifier, the one who in speaking always represents the zero, the nothing. He always stands as a shadow behind the events, but the beauty of it: he remains the shadow, he spends it when it becomes too bright.

Too bright from the too clever, the all-knowing, the 'Non Dupes' (the Not Stupid), who 'errent' (which err) as Lacan titled his XXI seminar. 'Les Nom du Père' (the names of the father), 'Les Non du Père' (the no of the father) and 'Les non Dupes errent' are all the same in French because of the homophony immanent there. This is how the language of the unconscious is structured, how the Formula Words are structured, and how the statement of Death is structured, scanded, shaped. "Be dupes," Lacan ,calls out to his listeners several times in this seminar. "Do not always be too much in the head, do not always understand everything too hastily and too quickly"! Also because the psychoanalyst often thinks he understands too directly the symptoms of his patient, he brings more resistance in finding the truth than the patient himself.

Nevertheless, in the 'Les non Dupes errent' you can also hear the jargon of death that always whispers something to you and you don't quite get it. That's why you have to turn it completely 'other way round' and know that the non-stupid ones, the pipsqueak ones, always go wrong, and that the father's no to the son (don't touch the mother), to his wife (don't eat the little ones), and to himself as proper name, logic determiner , is always there (even if it still has to be supplemented by 'visions'). Seen in this way, death is not the absolute master, neither with Mechthild nor with the one who struggles with *Analytic Psychocatharsis*, even if there is an absolute end somewhere, which is then longed for.

In the very next chapter, I want to show how Lacan brings the side of the image-acting, so favored by me, into the fabric of the psychoanalytic word-acting via the beautiful. He enters the beauty of love via the concept of the exciting, the exitative (an attenuated form of the Minne); with death, on the other hand, it is a matter of the true. It is enough to have seen him as what he - as described - is still able to do in living and love even after the medically determined death. In this deepest possibility of the regression one is not completely unconscious, as already mentioned the awareness differs from the consciousness.

Awareness must not necessarily be connected with these silly conscious, 'higher brain performances', one is also not completely unconscious in the dream. In the so-called lucid dream, which is not for nothing also called clear dream, one is even to a large extent conscious, about which I will report in the next chapter. By too many thoughts the awareness, which I distinguish therefore from the banal consciousness, is only darkened. Awareness can reach an important climax in the last phase of dying, it will be accompanied by something like a 'yes-that-is-it-experience', or simply by a self-affirming fusion with the Other, the A without a crossbar.

For this, minimal brain activities are sufficient, during which one does not have to be awake-conscious, which is mostly connected with the concept of consciousness, which - as mentioned - can also be called a pure mirror-consciousness. In deep sleep, on the other hand, there is an awareness about which nothing can be said, because it is easily overgrown by biological conditions. But in a good, mature, successful and finished meditation, these take a back seat to the experiences, events and concretistic image-word-acting made in the process. Therefore I can express it poetized with a 'that-is-it-experience', even if it is not as definite as it is said.

But this is a fundamental problem of the concept of awareness, which has more weight in the death-like state than in the everyday-labeling. The consciousness, which I have just determined in opposition to it, characterizes the distracted professor better, while the awareness, the real being-with-itself, can be thoughtless. One probably needs a procedure like the *Analytic Psychocatharsis* to fully understand this.

6. 'Leave him out'

Time for a graduated order. So the 'logical self-structure' is at the top, but obviously this has probably for most people only the appearance of a bare theory. However, with practice alone - although I strongly propagate it with the two exercises of *Analytic Psychocatharsis* - one does not get further either. That is why I have chosen the 'other way round' for the beginning - and that begins with the title on the cover and the heading of the first chapter of every book - especially that of love and death. This will not be completely strange to everyone, even if the 'other way round' may still remain a bit mysterious. Therefore I put once a scheme in the center where the corresponding terms are listed and their separating/connecting, the 'other way round', the real, is represented as a slash.

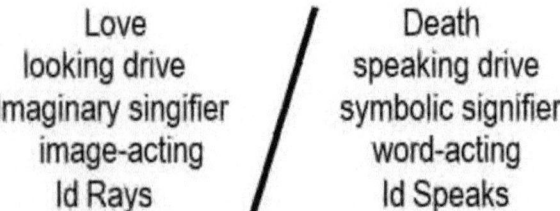

Love	Death
looking drive	speaking drive
imaginary singifier	symbolic signifier
image-acting	word-acting
Id Rays	Id Speaks

But now it should have become clear that the usual talk, ever even philosophical exaggerations of these two signifiers (I think they can be called that, even if neither of them takes precedence) is of no use. For Lacan, the signifier S1 was the master signifier. As mentioned, the first words were words of looseness or identity, which had a repeatedly expressed and commanding tone. Exactly, this makes the master, although this was initially only a simple man, whose speaking is close to death, as I already noted on several pages.

The man could assert himself only in such a way opposite the mothers and women that he started with a kind of voice power. He was the first to identify himself with the attacker, aggressor. R. Calasso, cultural historian and writer, writes that the first man crystallized when he still felt himself a member of an animalistic community, where everything was still mixed aggressively-sexually, but one had to defend oneself against the stronger and predatory animals. Finally one identified oneself with their strength and aggressiveness, and became so instead of the hunted oneself the hunter.[71] The philosopher C. Türcke also assumes that the "hominid hordes succeeded in repeating the horror of the forces of nature on their own instead of fleeing it".[72] The best example are the Neanderthals, who closely connected with storm and fire, with violence and hunt, ate enormous amounts of meat, whereby it also came to cannibalism. They did not get out of the master discourse.

---

[71] Calasso, R., Der himmlische Jäger (The heavenly Hunter), Suhrkamp (2020)
[72] Türcke, C., Nature and Gender, Critique of a Mania for Feasibility, C. H. Beck (2021)

To the 2nd signifier Lacan assigned knowledge, the knowledge, the simple 'now how'. According to Hegel, the servants were responsible for this and according to Freud and Lacan the women. This sounds discriminating and is also not quite logical in the last instance. That is why, in my view, the first two signifiers, the basic signifiers that also correlate to Freud's basic drives, the image-acting, to which I assign love, and the word-acting, which matches with death, are a closely entwined pair. I have already indicated the latter, the It Speaks, by telling about the constant talking past each other, about the ability to lie with words and the fundamental of language, to extinguish things in their originality, essence and power. Hegel, in any case, thought that the word was the murder of the thing. No sooner have we said: 'calmly lies there the lake in the sunlight', we have made the lake visible word-bound and even embellished it, but we have lifted it away from its many-founded spiritual side, we have cut it off, dried it up.

And lies and talking past and many other things - also my hopeless attempt to express something with words here - show even more how much the word-acting, the master-discourse, even logic is close to death. In contrast, love has something of the light-like image-acting, of the 'iconic', of the hidden knowledge. Only there it is really love, love in the knot itself as Lacan notes, in the imaginary-real where there is the actual enjoyment, the autochthonous, the feminine, the 'jouissance de l'Autre', which

Mechthild of Magdeburg was able to express so intensely; namely as a giving exactly in what one has and what it means to make a feast. A celebration out of the said nothing, the lack, the zero.

I too cannot explain what the 'other way round' of love and death are supposed to be. I know that both play a big role 'normally around', but they confuse thereby and confuse themselves. The 'other way round' rather gives them a chance, but everyone has to work it out for himself, fathom it psychoanalytically, practice it meditatively or experience it with the help of *Analytic Psychocatharsis*. I have derived the method of *Analytic Psychocatharsis* from linguistic, psychoanalytical, Lacanian and other scientific references; but this is only the outer framework. The personal way to it I have presented in a small brochure.[73] In short only this information: still during my psychoanalytic training I got to know the mediation teacher and religious scientist Kirpal Singh, whose method I learned. In the psychoanalytic institute they were not pleased at all.

They told me that psychoanalysis and meditation were not compatible. Particularly in tricky situations, one would then shift one into the other, would not, so to speak, continue the matter at hand consistently to the end or goal point. That was right, because I was fighting for

---

[73] Hummel, v., G., Die körperlich kranke Seele (The physically sick Soul) II, BoD (2012)

thirty years for the final correctness, for the final meaning and for the scientific clarity. In the meditation course I attended, old Sanskrit formulations were used, and I was often impressed how the participants of this method, whose groups I also attended in other countries (e.g. USA), reported positive results. All of them had improved and changed favorably, which I could not say so directly about myself.

Nevertheless, the matter was not difficult to understand. A prayer, for example, which aims for height, 'jouissance' and confirmation, benefits from intense faith, but has the disadvantage of always using the same or very similar content. In meditation, it is the other way round. One uses formulations which have no content, thus are foreign expressions, whereby the free thinking is reduced still more strongly as with the prayer, and thus height, 'jouissance' and confirmation turn out much more intensively. The disadvantage: there is no faith, so how do you convince yourself of the method? Well, there is also a certain transference effect. While the transference to the psychoanalyst is related to the fact that he is assumed to have knowledge, namely the knowledge that he would have about the nature of his patient from the beginning, in meditation one assumes that the meditation teacher has abilities, namely that he would have the right, special method for his adept at hand and would apply it.

However, something else was decisive for me, namely what then helped me to bring meditation and psychoanalysis together: The unconscious - according to Lacan - is ultimately a symbolic automatism, it is not about someone who speaks, but about It, the Freudian Id, the subject that Speaks (as the Other), that is, the 'phonetic rhythm' already mentioned by Leikert above.It is about that which can already be thematized in the usual use of language by the living and dead places of meaning, the signifiers. The empty, dead signifiers, which are also contained in a successful discussion or in the cooperation between analyst and patient, are, as mentioned, most feared by the lawyers, which is why they write long treatises with the most complicated formulations, only to make believe that everything is clearly stated.

But also otherwise people lose themselves in the beyond of an overdialectical and overartificial stilted vocabulary, which is hardly to communicate. Therefore it needed an explanation as concise as possible, almost mathematical, for these confusing connections of the symbolic automatism (which wants to stabilize the flood of images moved as if automatically by symbols, sounds, words). Lacan had marked this automatism, this 'sound rhythm' with the plus sign (+) for linguistic presence and the minus sign (-) for absence, and then formed further chains from alternating group distributions (+++ or ---, +-+ or -+-, then ++- , --+, -++, +--), so that a systematics corresponding to the symbolic emerged.

With it he wanted to show that before the usual language already protolanguage can be represented in abstract

form. I think much more simply one can see this phenomenon in meditations by using the sound experiences
made there as equally alternating, quieter, louder, ringing,
humming, resounding, throbbing, etc. to let them become
audible as the same proto-linguistic (a kind of hearing of
scarce thoughts, which however are not only fragments,
but scarce, phrase-like, but real thoughts). "Sound (spec.
in Chinese) is even one of the ways of proving the primacy of speech".[74] Lacan was brilliant sign logician of the
unconscious, and exactly the same I found only in the
meditation method I learned.

Thus, among the Sanskrit formulations I mentioned was
the word pair 'Sat Naam'. The root word Naam is the
same as in German Name, Latin nomen, ancient Indian
nama. It is also present in almost all languages, including
Finno-Ugric, "so that here is probably an ancient word".[75]
Moreover, this 'word' has numerous meanings in the various languages, but also within Indian: Naam, name,
word, designation, spirit, God, etc. The same applies to
the vocabulary Sat, which can mean being, essence, sin,
old Indian 'sits'. etc., and is also related to the Latin satis,
German satt. Very old and at the same time still today
valid words as well as words, which carry numerous
meanings, have always occupied the researchers. How

---

[74] Lacan, J., Seminaire XVIII, ed. Seuil, 5. Vortrag
[75] Kluge, F., Etymologisches Wörterbuch (Etymological Dictio-
nary) W. de Gruyter (1989) S. 498

was it possible to communicate in ancient Indian when some words combined so many meanings in one?

Freud has pointed out the essence of these primeval words, according to which even opposites like high / deep in Latin altus or profane / sacred in Latin sacer originate from an original meaning located in the unconscious. Altus meant some measure in the vertical, the space and width experience of the earlier people was obviously different than ours. Also the reported first words of the early men, the slogan words, were ambiguous and many-meaningful, but by functioning like a slogan word identity-determining, they got also again a uniqueness. There were fundamental identities in them. And so it was now no difficulty to understand why and how Sat Naam could function.

It was by a multiple meaning, by a - as Freud put it - "overdetermination", or even stronger evaluation coming from another source, capable of representing the (triadic or multiply structured) unconscious purely formally, primordially, purely from the linguistic stem![76] This was

---

[76] By stronger evaluation one can understand special oral traditions, tradition-boundness, mnemonics in scriptless cultures etc.. So there must not always be a purely linguistic overdetermination. But the identity embodying slogan character was given. Of course, it is still true that the positive transference to the teacher plays a major role in this. However, I will still show that it is precisely because of the ambiguous,

also the point of what was meant by Lacan's symbolic automatism. The different + and - chains are able (similar to the 0 1 digitalizations) to build complex information together. Somewhere in the middle, the simple names, formulas, syllabic words have their main functional value. In psychoanalysis one must go backwards, regress, to come back to the more elementary symbols, from which one can go forward again progressively interpreting.

The opposite, but equally structured, is the case with the meditation with Sat Naam and further Sanskrit formulations. Here the symbolic automatism of Lacan was already given, admittedly only a f o r m a l, thus nothing definitive. Thus such formulations stimulate equally the backward and forward step, an insight which now enabled me to elaborate the procedure of *Analytic Psychocatharsis*. For I now only had to find such formulations away from Sanskrit and to include them in the psychoanalytical explanations in order to get away from the mythical, mystical background lying above the meditation. I could now say that in the *Analytic Psychocatharsis* there is now a directly experienceable sound logic, music logic, in short: the logical original sound method of the unconscious.

---

linguistically knotted character of such a formulation that I can transform this factor into a scientifically justified usage.

An example: When I recently with the method of the *Analytic Psychocatharsis* myself the second exercise, in which one listens inwardly to exactly this sound rhythm, to the sound inside, above in the head right, I heard a phrase-like pass-word: " Den weglassen" (Leave him out)? What? Or even "Den Weg lassen" (letting the way - in German a Homophony). It's about exactly what the unconscious likes to do so much, namely to hide several meanings in the same formulation. I immediately thought of my formula words, and I also immediately had translations for the two described readings. The "letting the way" concerned above all my writing, my constant repetitions about the analytic-cathartic method and all the psychoanalytic commentaries. That all this could often be too high, too complicated, I thought again and again, and thus constantly considered whether I should not "leave this way".

But no, I should "leave him so". Now, on the other hand, there was also talk about "leaving out", and for this I associated much more strongly " him " whom I should "leave out", and this concerned a psychoanalytic colleague rivaling with me. The relationship track is usually the more significant one. I should "leave out him" who always disturbed my thoughts, this applied so clearly to me that there was no doubt. Only nobody told me that so clearly and definitely. Now I didn't talk to anyone about it either, but talking to yourself in an authentic and critical way is the best. The pass-words tell the truth, because they bring from the unconscious the other half of the truth to what one consciously considers as truth.

Of course, I don't have to leave everything out, and I must also be able to "leave the way as it is". But just maybe. Or should it be the 'iconic' that should be left out? No, that is what I want to add to psychoanalysis, or to bring it practically close to it. That was exactly what I couldn't talk about with my colleague. And also with Lacan not everything worked so simply. As mathematically and geometrically precise as Lacan's topologies are, they simply lack practice. An example from the life of P. Handke, who recently won the Nobel Prize for Literature, might help. A friend once asked him why Handke often entered the expression 'u. S.' in his diaries. That was an abbreviation for 'involuntary soliloquies,' Handke said sheepishly.[77] He writes down thoughts that come to him spontaneously, without warning, so to speak. It is not a conscious, linearly conceived process, a conscious reflection, nor just the usual creative ideas of the poet.

In a slightly pensive state, in which perhaps a few memories emerge, pale reminiscences, suddenly, as if coming from far away, strange words mix into the thinking. They are not sober, lifeless, inauthentic thoughts. One can take them up, and by having already grasped this thought as belonging to one, one expands it to a soliloquy, which is

---

[77] Kümmel, P., Was bedeutet ‚u.' ‚S.' ?, DIE ZEIT vom 2. 12. 19.

now of course of a completely different kind than the conscious, arbitrary soliloquies, which probably everyone has once. When I read this story by Handke, my immediate association was that this u. S. fit perfectly with the explanation of the pass-words in *Analytic Psychocatharsis*.

Handke could just as well have accomplished it with *Analytic Psychocatharsis*. There the formula-words are the language of love the ' other way round ', because normally no lover speaks such a coded language. Death, on the other hand, is awakened by his 'other way round'. He likes the symbolic automatism, which he transforms into reasonably understandable phrases towards the pass-words. By braking the normally linguistic, susceptible to lies, he expresses meanwhile all the more the truth. Certainly, the phrase with the 'den weglassen' is not a profound or highly spiritual statement. One could always think of it that way. Also the everyday consumer will often feel that leaving out this or that is better than taking more and more. It must not always be completely clear.

Still, an essential trait of Pass-Words is their timbre emerging so surprisingly, authentically and overwhelmingly from the unconscious. The phrases are often so breathed, quiet but clear. Because they don't assault you in the midst of other activities, but are merely nudged by an independent exercise like in the *Analytic Psychocatharsis* oriented to Lacan's psychoanalysis, they simply have a more serious effect. There is something original in them that one believes. One can doubt them, but at the same time one considers the ulterior meaning, which, with some knowledge from psychoanalysis, but also from an honesty towards oneself, represents the essential to the contribution of self-maturation. The pass-words are really also identity words.

As has now been shown several times, also here, that is, with regard to the concept of 'overdetermination' or the living and dead signifiers, St. Mechthild provides a simple and concise formula. For the Trinity also represents a 'superdetermination,' but Mechthild does not see it as an abstract, theological construct. She understands it as truly real, as a game of minne: "The minne game of the divine Trinity [...] is thus not alone [...] a relaxing enjoyment of God, rather the game, if it is to be perfect, is based on a partnership and common dynamic between the forms of being and being of God and his soul.[78] And further by another author: "Thus the love immanent to the being creates an object for itself, God himself is the 'victim of his lust, therefore logically also of his eroticism and finally of his passion', as the scientist S. Buholzer remarks on it".[79]

---

[78] Driller, J., Innaugural dissertation, Gaben und Gegengaben (Gifts and Countergifts) im Werk der Mechthild von Magdeburg, Universität-Gesamthochschule Paderborn, 2005.

[79] Buholzer, S., A., Studies on the Concept of God and Soul in the Work of Mechthild of Magdeburg, Peter Lang InternationaloAcademicoPublisherso(1988) p.112

There we have it again, Mechthild's image-acting Minne-practice dominates the cumbersome, academic theory, which Lacan had to produce by word-acting with his Bo-Knot and braid in long-winded tirades. Both have their full justification, but precisely because of their opposition, an overarching third is needed, which I attempt to establish with *Analytic Psychocatharsis*. Although the method of *Analytic Psychocatharsis* is described in detail in the appendix, here is a brief preliminary remark. In the first exercise, initially with closed eyes, attention is paid to an inwardly occurring It Rays ('trickling through', lucidity), while at the same time three to five formula words are repeated one after the other purely in thought. If the resulting catharsis (liberating, dissolving) is clear enough (or even after twenty minutes of application), one switches to the second exercise.

In this exercise one concentrates on the inner sound, on the Id Speaks, on the right side of the head (reference to the temporal side of the brain). If you listen long enough, the sound inside becomes a phrase, a pass-word like the one just described with 'leave him out". A short intellectual check of the meaning in the sense of psychoanalytic theory may be appropriate, but mostly the meaning of the pass-word is immediately clear to the person concerned. I will give other examples and explanations in the following. Further, as said, in the appendix.

7. Visions 'the other way round'

To my thesis of the 'other way round' I mention again the book of the science journalist S. Klein.[80] He proved that already with the earliest humans, yes the hominids or primates, the creative, inventive activity was present, which goes along with a certain imagination. In this sense also already the ants have imagination, because they must have invented by always new developments - one could almost say - of planning nature their highly complex state system. As remembered, Damasio called this mind/spirit, while I spoke of naive consciousness, which does not yet know awareness (awareness of the complexity of existence and resting in the context of truth and knowledge). One can support Damasio's view, of course, by the function of niche formation singled out by evolutionary theory. Animals found a niche in their world (inconspicuousness through smallness, organization formation, etc.) through which they could expand.

With the hominids this niche consisted in the more complex brain, but for the creativity it was enough that it was only one third as large or as with the Neanderthals much less interlaced as that of the today's humans. According to my thesis this was even advantageous, even if the fur-

---

[80] Klein, S., Wie wir die Welt ändern (How we are changing the world), S. Fischer (2021).

ther development - also by S. Klein - is always described as a great, progressive, higher-spiritual main cerebrum-formation. In my opinion it is only a further development in the external success, in the cultic, technical, manipulative, but not a bit of real progress in the awareness, which is progress just in the mentioned creativity, imagination and creative activity. Apart from the fact that we still have Neanderthal genes in us, we have not really gained anything in awareness, so for example in this experience fact of the connection of an 'other way round' of love and death. On the contrary, the meanwhile by many people as grotesque, hypertrophic, manically degenerated over-civilization, over-technicization and now also over-digitalization means with regard to the creativity, the imagination and awareness of each individual an enormous step backwards.

The small or the little networked brains have still possessed the ability for the awareness of the life fulfillment in dying, the love as an enchantment of death, the death as a stirrup holder of the enjoying substance, the 'jouissance' and many other things more (concerning the creative). Today, one staggers among thousands of flashes, snippets of language, nonsense information, fake news, etc.,. Anyway, I don't want to become an eternityist and only want to convey that the imagination mentioned by S. Klein, this primarily creative, is exactly the 'iconic', which I have already tried several times. Although I always explained that it is not free of something self-derived, which in itself does not necessarily - like the 'tree' or even the 'sea' - serve a final meaningful purpose . But it has minne, especially when it comes together with the 'rhetorical'.

So I have returned to small-brainedness and allowed myself a trip to the primeval times in the form of a 'vision' of the sea. Like the 'mountain' and the 'tree' and many other mystical quantities, the 'sea' belonged to it. After a short time of the first, more meditative exercise of the *Analytic Psychocatharsis*, this 'vision' sometimes appears to me. It comes to a cathartic shimmering, this time almost self-made as a primordial view, as a fully set in motion imagination of the vastness and blueness of the sea. The fascination is immensely greater than the real view of a seascape, which I have often had on some beaches or coastal regions, which has also often been great. But now it was just like the early hominids must have experienced it.

Because they have not only known the 'sea' in these primeval times in the best way, all life has originated in it, but also loved, sanctified. They have minned it as Mechthild would say.[81] Already there, with the earliest unicellular organisms, and certainly better comprehensible with the first humans, there has already been creativity and the autochthonous enjoyment with regard to the

---

[81] I write 'sea' in quotation marks, if it is not only about the real water masses, but also and especially in connection with it, about the 'vision sea'.

'sea'. Already there they have swum in it - already from the look -, have bathed visually in its enjoyment and 'flowing rhythm'.[82] Lacan meant that the enjoyment is a characteristic of the living par excellence, i.e. that it behaves also with the plants in such a way that they enjoy.[83] Trees, amoebae, and bacteria also enjoy, he asserted.[84] "The substance of all kinds of enjoying, in fact, borders on suffering, and this is the dress by which it is recognized - if the plant did not suffer manifestly, we would not know that it was alive."[85]

This most original enjoyment, which is inherent even in the flora, the fauna and even in the 'sea', concerns the access to the primary creative, as S. Klein postulates, and it seems to be so elementary and just primordial that people today have largely repressed, forgotten or discarded it. Many authors start now for this reason to look for the life even in the driest matter as for example E. Coccia or Jane Bennet. The latter author's central thesis is that "matter is active - and it even has political agency at times. . . . When should this statement [that matter is alive] be more plausible than today, when a small virus

---

[82] I remind once again that Lacan used the term 'flowing rhythm' to refer to feminine enjoyment, to the feminine Eros.

[83] Lacan, J., Lettres de L'Ècole freudienne, Nr. 16 (1975) S. 192

[84] Lacan, J., Seminar XXI, Lecture from 23. 4. 1974.

[85] Lacan, J., Seminar XVIII, Vortrag vom 17. 3. 1971

has the whole world on tenterhooks?[86] "Is not the virus the prototype of the viral material, in that we can disassemble it into its RNA, spike proteins, and its molecules, just as we can disassemble a Harley Davidson, but the virus then develops the most idiosyncratic vivacity, so it acts"?[87]

I don't think you can say things that way, because what do people get out of this reality addiction? I admit that if one asks about the relation to the animal world, to vegetarianism and to what W. Hellpach calls geopsyche and E. Gartmann called ecopsychoanalysis, would have to include many areas in my 'Visions' concept. For both the 'living matter' and the through-psychologized fauna and flora would have to be considered by psychoanalysis. But where would it get there? It is true that it lacks, as has been said often enough now, the better inclusion of the imaginary-real, of the image-acting into the overall concept. The occupation with linguistics, with the symbolic, word-acting is exhausting enough for the procedure of classical psychoanalysis, but one should mention - especially with regard to full awareness - the ecopsychoanalytic.[88] Ethnopsychoanalysis is also practiced, and that -

---

[86] Bennett, J., Vibrant Matter: A Political Ecology of Things, John Hope Franklin Center Book (2010)

[87] Roedig, A., Deutschlandfunk Kultur, Lesart vom 25.6. 2020

[88] Köhler-Weisker, A., Conversations under the Mopane Tree, Ethnopsychoanalytic Encounters with Himbanomads, psychosozial Verlag (2015).

even if problematic again - not without success. The fulfilling awareness increases all this in any case, but this becomes possible probably only in an own procedure as for example the *Analytic Psychocatharsis*.

Back to the sea and to my kind of 'sea' psychoanalysis. I remember an evening in La Spezia, somewhat tired from a long drive, near the harbor, fifty meters from the pier and already dark: far outside a light, just a dot, sparkling across like a late promise, promise of delight, promise of happiness. But the inner, iconic view into the vastness of the sea, into the tiny lucidity of Freud's representation of imagination, into the luminescent 'vision', is incomparably more fantastic, more real, more soulful. But for this, for this awareness, one needs a not too big brain, the imagination alone is enough. One needs One more, this true One, in which the 'sea' is not only reflected, but wildly, thunderously, foamingly heightened, as in Nolde's painting with the title 'Sea 1' (which contains One more, because Nolde painted this ecstatic sea shown on the cover many times).

Undoubtedly, in this painting Nolde strives to transcend the sea, perhaps into the 'iconic' or even further. For one sees only a wave breaking and in the background often the gilded sky. Nolde's numerous sea paintings are almost always about this spiritualization, over-awareness, the 'other way round' of love for the sea and of death through the intertwining of the waves, usually painted in deep darkness. It is not about a picture, it is about a 'vision' that seduces the viewer by means of an eye deception: rather look at the picture before you get lost in the real 'vision' of the 'sea' (as I have described it).[89]

The driving force, which in Freud's case is heading for its goal only in a roundabout way (outburst of affect, defense mechanisms, compulsion to think, etc.), is in the case of the mentioned 'visions' much more immediate, overwhelming and is thus close to the hallucinations. And yet it is also well distinguished from them, just as it can be clearly distinguished from neurological phenomena, e.g. so-called uncinate seizures'. Such seizures, which are close to epilepsy, often impress by their fascinating perceptual and gustatory experiences, but are purely neurological-pathological in nature. In contrast, the 'iconic visionary' can be understood as a mixture of the consciously and unconsciously psychic, which could likewise be experienced in earlier cultures and religious experiences, in ecstatic rituals and states of intoxication. Through the formula-words, however, the 'iconic' is al-

---

[89] Blümle, C., Von der Heiden, A., Blickzähmung und Augentäuschung (Gaze Taming and Eye Deception), diaphanes (2005). "Because the image is that appearance which claims to be that which gives appearance, Plato stands up against painting as an activity that rivals his. This other is the psychic object 'small a', the curiosity, for which a battle is waged, whose soul is the deception of the eye" (Lacan).

ways kept at a clear visual distance and also at a logical distance for the following pass-words.

Thus calmer, more assured, more composed, I follow in this 'iconic' of the 'sea' and the immeasurable expanse, going beyond the waves, higher and higher, further and further. At some point I break off, maybe already after a few minutes, because I don't want to depend on these lucid moments. Mechthild also writes that you don't want to linger too long in the single rapture. "in the rapture I saw a mountain [she also had such an experience!], that happened very suddenly. For no body could bear for the soul to be there for an hour".[90] She suspects the phallic nature of the mountain, and that is not the point. The Minne is meant for the beloved and no one else, while I consider the literal revelation in the pass-words as the main goal. For Mechthild it is already enough to hear only his voice.

If behind the 'sea' the narrow fringe of a distant country would appear (because I can't control all this myself and freely, as much as I get the sparkling glimmer of myself in the inner view with the thought of the 'sea'), this would perhaps awaken my curiosity for the landscape and the people at this unknown shore. Strange people, beautiful people, bodies, eyes and God knows what other figures could appear, and that brings no one anything. Or?

---

[90] Mechthild von Magdeburg, The Flowing Light of the God-head, Publishing House of World Religions (2010) II, 21

Again: I exclude horror scenarios, because in this respect the *Analytic Psychocatharsis* is too much determined by the character of the scientifically built up formula-words and the rationally interpretable pass-words.

If one would not have this clear guidance, one could certainly fall into nightmare-like 'visions', as they had to experience the still wildly and uncontrolled meditating mystics and hermits a la Saint Anthony, who famously withdrew several times into the desert, where he was haunted by agonizing horror scenarios. Ugly grimaces, wild animals and monster figures haunted him. The painter Max Ernst depicted these mental tortures very well and even won the first prize for it in a competition. Antonius is said to have lived to be a hundred and four years old, despite or because of his asceticism and hallucinations. This is also said of many Old Testament figures, of Buddha and Indian saints.

For freely I must add that the 'sea' fits well with what in psychoanalysis is called the 'preoedipal mother'.It is represented in the Oedipus saga by the Sphinx, in the ancient Orient by the maternal Ishtar, and in modern man by the ecstatic, neurotic or perverse in the unconscious core phantasm. This phantasm contributes decisively to the forms of desire and longing of modern man, but one cannot completely do without such a phantasm in the form of the 'iconic' just for a full, plump life-formation. Freud believed to be able to do without it in the turning away from hypnosis, in which, as reported, the patients gave themselves up to catharsis, but I use in the *Analytic Psychocatharsis* for the jump from the 'vision' to the 'rhetoric' the pass-word the catharsis in a constructive way. If one has the cathartic leap in mind, one will not dwell long on the 'sea' and the uncontrolled side of the preoedipal mother'.

A vivid example for the preoedipal are the giant and tons heavy statues on the Easter Island. They do not represent mother figures, but probably - as extensively researched - forebodings on which regional rulers based themselves in each case.[91] However, they undoubtedly have something 'iconic' about them, as do many other sculptures, architectures and works of art like the Egyptian pyramids, the Mona Lisa or Beethoven's music. In all of them there is the imaginary-real dazzle that we nevertheless do not want to miss, just as the inhabitants of Easter Island did not want to do without their monumental figures.

The figures must have fascinated the islanders enormously, but it was precisely this fascination, this also political grandstanding of the VIPs on the island, that they finally succumbed to in the sense of a preoedipal lust. They needed an enormous amount of wood to erect and transport the figures. For this and other reasons, they deforested the island to such an extent that animals, plants, climate, etc., did not recover and the entire island

---

[91] Diamond, J., Collapse, How Societies Choose to Fail or to Survive (2011)

society perished. They lost themselves in the images, sounds and monuments of power.

The author J. Diamond already pointed out years ago with this narration the parallelism to the today's time and its global situation of the climate and environment. Of course, he argues that today there is a greater overview and more numerous technical methods available to avoid such a fate on the whole planet. Finally, the inhabitants of Easter Island were also largely isolated for centuries. But Diamond cannot give a plausible solution. Finally, the imaginary-real is too boundless. Moreover in the meantime everyone knows that for a solution of the environmental and climate problems one would have to motivate specifically the individual.

Though I want to report about a self-analytical procedure, I want to inspire a science of the subject, a coming-together for each individual who needs it or is interested in it, even if one first dives into 'visions'. As I said at the beginning, the word, the term 'vision' is actually wrong. It seduces to mysticism, but the activation of catharsis, which as reported Freud could no longer use, has a neutral, liberating character and is thus extremely useful in the *Analytic Psychocatharsis* in the transition (Lacan: tranformation) to the revealing pass-word. I have already emphasized this moment and I emphasize it again. Indeed, if Lacan claims that in mysticism the signifier answers to itself, this does not apply to *Analytic Psychocatharsis*. In the transition (from the first to the second exercise) a process of transformation takes place, an 'other way round' of the signifiers, which keeps the significant movement in a continuous train, but uses precisely the 'défilé signifiant' to jump. Just in the 'other way round' lies the 'défilé'.

Now one does not have to choose only the 'sea' or the beautiful people, three rings twisted in themselves, the Bo-Knot, an endogenous formation, a 'star', small circles, 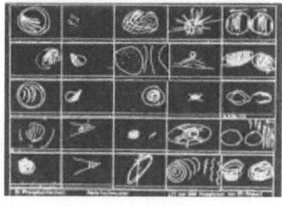 would also do it (see illustration above), in order to give content to the 'iconic'.[92] Then, of course, something else happens. The rings will not irritate, they will open and close. Quite automatically, thread formations similar to those painted by Lacan will emerge, as well as other geometric figures, such as were also inspired by constellations in the past, even though I would like to keep the distance to astrological or arbitrary images here. Whether they are small dots and circles, the important thing is that the catharsis comes about, from which one can then start the transformation to the second exercise. Without such a momentum, the pass-word usually does not open enough.

---

[92] Eichmeier, J., Höfer, O., endogen image patterns, U&S - Verlag (1974), which can be produced by stimulation of upstream visual areas, but here impress as not meaningful because of their simplicity and so.

But when it opens, the short phrases, the sayings come about, which - as Lacan also demanded for psychoanalysis - can go to the limit of wisdom. Wisdom, "la sagesse," he asked, namely, "c'est quoi," what is it? . "C'est le savoir de la 'jouissance', it is the knowledge of enjoying", namely the knowledge of the very last, autochthonous enjoying.[93] Lacan even says of it that this ultimate 'jouissance' - in its most comprehensive and superordinate way, so to speak - is the "enjoyment of the real that goes together with the real of enjoyment," which can only be explained with a reference to love.[94] It is, in fact, that has such a difficult stand in psychoanalysis, because it is precisely related to this 'iconic', image-acting, the Rays, and thus resists the symbolic, word-acting (which has to do with death). Only in the concrete context of the two does the real and its enjoyment come fully into play.

Lacan suggests this, at any rate, in the cited Seminar XXI. He starts from the mirroring love, from the love for one's own image on the one hand and from that for the Other, that is then the one without the crossed out A, which Freud connected with this peculiar father of the prehistoric times. Love, however, remains unexpressible in it, but Lacan attests to it an excitement ('passionnant', 'excitant') that is exactly the same that I tried to convey with the 'iconic' of the 'mountain' and the 'sea'. This love

---

[93] Lacan. J., Seminaire XIX, seuil (2011) S. 169
[94] Lacan, J., Seminar XXI, Vortrag vom 12. 3. 1974

is not passive, Lacan writes, the stupid thing is that in psychoanalysis one has to try to dissolve this little love, which as mentioned is called transference love, because it is related to the transference of significances onto the therapist, which are just inadequate, not really appropriate or extremely complicated to look at.

But since love can be exciting, captivating, 'passionnant', or perhaps is even fundamental, it also has to do with 'jouissance', and here Lacan sees a way out of the dilemma of love, which can so quickly slide into the totally imaginary, maternal, romanticizing, rapturous, even into the false, ideological, confessional and completely deceptive. For only the love, which is connected with the knowledge of enjoyment, can lead out of the jam. As already discussed above, lovers have only half the knowledge, and the solution consists in the fact that – as Lacan complained – one must "invent the knowledge" in the true, accurate, actual love. One invents it by giving it a body. It is the body already given in concession to death and already marked by it. It is the body of bodily images joined together in itself.

It is not, then, the purely material body, it is a body without form, the body in meditation, one that is "made of the consistency of bodily images," with respect to which Lacan says that it is by definition a 'substance jouissante,' the substantial enjoying already cited, which contrasts with the substantial thinking of Descartes and the substantial extended of Aristotle. With this, love steps out of the merely mirroring "glorification of the body" and is more concerned with its truth, with its consistent truth. Indeed, to take the example of psychoanalysis again, it is a matter of "in what way truth touches the psychoanalyst himself, . . because, after all, it is there that truth gets its primary meaning, because - what I have been pointing out for a long time" - and here Lacan now really turns the argumentation the 'other way round', "because there is only a transference of the analyst himself, because ultimately he is the subject that is supposed to know."[95] He is supposed to be the Other, the 'other way round' of love and death, which knows everything that is at stake in the psychic.

Not only is he assumed to know, "he should also know," Lacan went on to say, "how he conceives himself in his relation to knowledge, to what extent it is determined by the unconscious structure that separates him from this knowledge, although of course he knows something about it. And I emphasize this, as much by the test he has made in his own analysis as by what he has seen in his own life, in his own analysis as by what my statement can bring him. Does that mean that the transference is the entrance to the truth? It is the entrance to something that is the truth, but the truth whose transmission is precisely the discovery: the truth of love".[96]

---

[95] Lacan, J., Seminaire XXI, Lecture from 19. 3. 1974
[96] Lacan, J., Seminaire XIX, seuil (2011)

In *Analytic Psychocatharsis*, these aspects are to be seen in the same way, for what Lacan emphasizes also concerns this 'other way round' of love, which also has to do with the 'other way round' of death. "It is, after all, the case that every half-narrative of the true has death as its principle, because the true is something with which analytic experience can bring us into contact . . .the true cannot be defined otherwise than as that which in sum drives the body toward 'jouissance,' and that in it that which compels it to do so is nothing other than the principle by which sex is very concretely connected with the death of the body."

"Only in sexual beings does the body die. And this compulsion to reproduce is indeed served by the little we can say that is true. I will say even more, since it is about death. . . For we have always only the true resemblance, because this death, the principle of the true, this death in the speaking being, while it speaks, is never anything but a deception. To have death really before one's eyes is not within the reach of the true. Death pushes it before itself.To have it in front of you, to have to deal with death, that only happens within the framework of the beautiful, in the aesthetics of love, where it touches emotionally."

"I've demonstrated this before when I did The Ethics of Psychoanalysis, and it's touching, why? Because things are in a certain rotational order, it makes a difference in that it [the beautiful] glorifies the body: there the princi-

ple is 'jouissance.'[97]   But not only there, because as Lacan explained just before, this is equally true with regard
to the truth of love, in that in this respect we are "playing
a game whose rules we do not know". It is about the
game with knowledge in love and the connection with
death.

"And so if this knowledge must be invented in order for
there to be knowledge, then perhaps that is what psychoanalytic discourse can serve. Only, if it's true that 'what
we gain on one side, we lose on the other,' then surely
there's something that jumps out. It's not hard to find:
What jumps out is 'jouissance'. For in this blind thing we
do under the name of love, there is no lack of 'jouissance'! We have plenty of it! The wonderful thing is that
we know nothing about it, but perhaps it is precisely in
the nature of 'jouissance' that we can never know anything about it."

Lacan must speak so cryptically, because he does not
know this intensive practice, which plays the main role in
the *Analytic Psychocatharsis* and which simplifies everything a little, in that especially there the cryptically remained shows itself, it can also be 'seen' and experienced
practically and confirmed by pass-words also with the
logic of the unconscious. Also I repeat this already for the
umpteenth time. The 'iconic', the image-acting, the pure

---

[97] Lacan, J., Seminar XXI, Lecture from 12. 3. 1974

Id Rays, the 'other way round of love and death, the 'jou-issance', all that needs just also the 'rhetorical', the word-acting, the Id Speaks, finally, however, a successful, mature, real connection, combination of the two: theoretically in the Bo-Knot, practically in the exercises of the *Analytic Psychocatharsis*.

Just the practical relations are also indicated in the so-called lucid dream, which recently is already offered to the general public for therapeutic purposes.[98] There, too, picture events, transformations and mergings take place, on which one has a certain influence from a semiconscious state, so that besides the imaginary, the picture-acting, which actually radiates in the lucid dream by means of a direct reference to the body pictures, also word-acting can come to the fore. If the body images are very strongly intertwined, this catharsis of lucidity, which is very slightly under current, is generated.

One is in the lucid dream word-mentally in the position to steer the appearing scenes somewhat. There exists an enormous amount of literature, adventurous and more scientific kind next to each other about this phenomenon also called lucid dream. I used to experience lucid dreams myself, that is, at the beginning of my exercises with *Analytic Psychocatharsis*. One has a certain awareness -

---

[98] Knab, B., Gerhard, S., Im Schlaf zur Erholung (During sleep to rest), ZEIT-online, 26. 7. 2017

most people mistakenly say consciousness - of the fact that one is dreaming - and a half-awareness, which I always understood only as a particularly intense state of meditation. I knew every time in these dreams: now I am again in this vision-like moment and can glide over landscapes, experience the most intense lightness, see great colors and primeval things, but I was always annoyed afterwards or the next morning that I had not thought of anything else or had not thought of the actual meditation formulas, which would have brought me much further.

Even if the landscapes were fantastic and appeared very similar to what I called 'iconic', I always had an unclear intention that I should strive for a 'higher', a 'higher out', but I was always afraid that I would get too close to the sun like Icarus and that I would not be able to stand the heat. A probably quite childlike, intuitive reflex, but at the same time a proof for the fact that one does not have the whole view in the lucid dream. After all, I was lying comfortably in bed and didn't need to be afraid of suffering the fate of Icarus. That shows the problem.

I can explain the essence of the 'lucid dream' with the total mirror world of the joined body image. In the normal dream the body images move a little bit together under the primacy of the sleep desire, but also of a psychophysical exhaustion, almost without consciousness and awareness.[99] In the lucid dream, however, the closer connection of the body images remains for a while. The "solipsism of the dream" is, as the dream researcher D. Wyss thought, especially in its lucid form not yet completely caught up by the "opposing reality of waking", so that only a reduced thinking is possible, a half-conscious trance thinking, which nevertheless cannot be a basis for a science of the subject.[100] But as the thoughts about the lucid phenomena have the character of proximity to the unconscious, the two basic forces, the Rays and Speaks are definitely in play again, but still combined in a rather uncontrolled way.

Their combination, their 'lowest combination' (a term from R. Musil's novel 'The Man Without Eyes') is completely unsteady and disordered and thus unsuitable for a therapeutic procedure. The Chinese philosopher Chuang-Tse fared a little better, dreaming to be a butterfly and waking up wondering if it was not a butterfly dreaming to be a human being. According to Lacan, "He is right, in two respects, because, first, it proves that he is not crazy, he does not consider himself absolutely identical with Chuang-Tse, and secondly, because he is not aware that

---

[99] A certain implied awareness exists in the dream in that it represents an unconscious desire as fulfilled, but one experiences it as really fulfilled, which is not the ultimate awareness.
[100] Wyss, D., Traumbewusstsein (dream consciouness), Vanden-hoeck und Ruprecht (1988) S. 165-179

he is hitting the bull's-eye so precisely with his statement. In fact, when he was just butterfly, he grasped himself at a root of his identity, he was and is in his essence this butterfly, painting himself in his own colors . . but this does not mean that he is captured by the butterfly, he is captured butterfly, but prey of nothing, because in the dream he is nobody's butterfly. When he wakes up, he is Chuang-Tse for the others and is caught in their butterfly net".[101]

He is wrapped up in the net of the general Id Rays / Speaks, whose slant makes him waver, irritated. But he does not leave it at that: like Socrates, he begins to philosophize and thus to step out of the simple butterfly existence and the equally simple I-am-I, out of his pure fluttering shell-name. He asks himself, like J. Bennett, about the 'living matter', about the nature/human unity and why this is so difficult to achieve. Because from the moment when everybody shouts in his ear: Chuang Tse, Chuang Tse! he is again only that cipher which all people give themselves with and against each other. He must create a philosophy or psychoanalysis that goes beyond that, but preserves his butterfly!

Between sleep and reality there is therefore no clearly delimitable intermediate stage, only in meditation, in

---

[101] Lacan, J. The Four Basic Concepts of Psychoanalysis, Seminar XI, Walter, (1980) p. 82.

psychoanalysis, in the lucid dream, etc., one can move as it were like on a third platform, which is different in each case.In the lucid dream it succeeds for some time to summarize the body images and characters and to hold them stable, so that one can hold together waking and dreaming just not in the freedom-significant, but in the somewhat directed, meditative or in Freud's 'equally floating attention' similar state. But it remains predominantly with the banal mirror experience.

Freud called the pure self-image mirroring the "primary narcissism", an aspiration to lucid self-love, self-lighting, to an 'egoism of light' as some yoga teachers say. One must think of the happening in the sense of Einstein's geometry (topology), in which just the infinite straight line comes back into the finite and is thereby equivalent to the circle. But the circle is an early and decisive form of the imaginary signifier and this not only because one puts it as a ring on the finger or puts it as a chain around the neck. Also the moon and sun disk and many other ring forms belong to the signifier supplied by nature, which symbolize the in itself closed, connecting, thus the transition from the imaginary to the linguistic and back again, the beginning of a consolidating order, which is however no absolutely effective, no usable real.

The lucid dreamer, the philosopher, the imaginator, indeed often the painter of art, lacks the word-acting reassurance of who he himself really is, human and butterfly, I and Other. In all these esoteric and lucid dreaming attempts one always comes to a point where one becomes completely irrational, which is also possible in the waking state when one thinks something paranoid. The paranoiac absolutely does not consider himself to be paranoid. The lucid dreamer doesn't notice that a healthy desire to sleep leads him back to Morpheus when the dream tissue becomes too nonsensical, the philosopher doesn't notice that people don't follow him when the too many thoughts rush over and the art painter doesn't notice when he only seduces to the 'eye deception'.

The explanation of my method, the *Analytic Psychocatharsis*, can best be created with Lacan's 'défilés signifiantes', the significant constrictions. For the formula-words are nothing else than such a logical, significant 'défilé', through which one has to pass in order to reach the goal. The 'visions' are also such narrowings, which can lead one through the inflation of the figurative. One only has to coordinate both of them appropriately. Thus, in the first exercise of the *Analytic Psychocatharsis*, the 'défilé' is built up by the fact that the word-acting of the formula-words (*Speaks*) clears the way for the boundless image-acting (*Rays*) by the overdetermination and the thus mediated impossibility of any sense but exactly following the essence of the Other and thus correctly delimited.

But as soon as the *Rays* has oscillated over all appearances ('mountain', 'tree', 'sea') to the cathartic point of lucidity, the second exercise of listening inwardly returns to the word-acting and opens itself - now freed from the overde-termination - to the pass-words. All the science writers I have quoted lack this combination of 'vision/rhetoric' with regard to that what could be a formula of the sub-ject. Always one side or the other comes up short. Or the 'lowest conflation' of the two does not succeed. But all this is different in *Analytic Psychocatharsis*, which is why in the next chapter I will describe a short version of the method, which is more about the practical part. With this description and a small supplement in the appendix, it should be possible for everyone to start with the two simple exercises of the method from study alone.

8. Lacan's 'Thing' and the Awareness of Mechthild of Magdeburg

I give a final summary of what has often been repeated in fragments so far. From the beginning I have distinguished consciousness from awareness. Consciousness is merely a mirrored perception of the world into an inner substrate, for example in specific areas of the brain. The neuroscientist G. Tononi created such a modern theory of consciousness.[102] According to him, "the degree of consciousness depends on the structure of the underlying substrate: the more coherent a substrate is, the more conscious is it. According to this theory, cognition would therefore by no means be limited to living beings", two other scientists write in the Spektrum der Wissenschaft regarding Tononi's concept.[103] And: "Thus, one can also assign a certain degree of consciousness to a circuit, a computer or a stone - even if it may be very small".

The scientists also point to Damasio and his three levels of consciousness: proto-self, core consciousness and expanded consciousness, all of which fail to capture actual awareness. Even in Damasio's extended consciousness

---

[102] Tononi, G. et al., Integrated information theory: From consciouness to its physical substrate. Nature Reviews Neuroscience 17 (2016)

[103] Krauß, P., Maier, A., Bewusstsein (consciousness), Spektrum der Wissenschaft 7 (2021) S. 12-20

the emphasis is again on the typical 'higher cognitive functions', already smugly caricatured by me, on the conscious access to brain and language, thus far from the fulfilling awareness. This is connected with a far-reaching self-sublimation into the 'iconic' (or elementary Rays / Speaks). If one reads through the recent literature on the question of the conscious and the unconscious, this difference is still hardly elicited. On the contrary, one sees increasingly in the artificial intelligence the deciding competitor to the human consciousness. But who will be so Manichean and reach for the machines!

Thereby Tononi's approach is not bad at all, because it shows that for the stone this distinction consciousness / awareness does not apply yet, only something consciousness-like already starts with it. In the higher cognitive states, however, one would have to ask about the "number of all possible mental states in the human brain (substrate) concerning the substrate", the mentioned authors write in the Spektrum der Wissenschaft, and this would then become completely absurd. The consciousness would become violently ill at too much of itself. Thus, nevertheless, it becomes clear that at a certain stage between stone and the infinity of mental states, one has to get out of the substrate in time, to take off self-sublimating or to speak fuzzilogically like Lacan, in order to get to what can be called the full awareness, which can be clearly separated from the bland consciousness.

This is also confirmed by the authors in the article in the Spektrum der Wissenschaft, reporting on 'eliminativism', a psychological research direction where "the mind is fully functional even without consciousness". It is astonishing that neuroscientists go so far and obviously also refer to the phenomenon of awareness, because what should be 'fully functional mind without awareness'? Exactly, exclusive awareness! One can represent the whole perhaps a little more descriptively on the basis of the example of the intermediate realm of death. There only the small consciousness of the stone prevails, or let's say: of the prokaryotes (unicellular organisms without cell wall). If the people therefore complain that the one who is in the intermediate realm does not consciously perceive anything anymore, can never wake up and is in the final stage without any possibility for 'higher cognitive performances', they are absolutely right.

But it is also in the extreme state of regression and elimination, which psychoanalysis regards as unconscious, but it does so because it conceives the unconscious - especially according to Lacan - as "structured like a language, like the language of the Other". It can be about the quoted 'logical automatism', in whose primary speaking there is also more awareness than consciousness. And the radiant can be ultrasubjective - as Lacan notes - and that is, as with the ecstatic, exist outside of consciousness, but reside all the more in the fulfilling awareness which some are so fond of naming it 'spiritual'. In the word- and image-acting, in the Speaks and in the Rays, consciousness and awareness cannot always be clearly distinguished. Mechthild of Magdeburg had an easier work in this regard.

For Mechthild of Magdeburg, consciousness is precisely that which is grasped intellectually from the outside through understanding, while awareness is that which is acquired from within, so to speak, by grace (spontaneously, meditatively, self-sublimated). The grace, the minne, all these strongly charged, elevated and from considerable self-sublimation originating quantities make clear distinctions possible for her. She must, however, purchase them dearly. Minne, for example, has a clear erotic-sexual underpinning, which is, after all, what caused the Catholic Church not to canonize Mechthild (those compulsive neurotic pettifoggers!). And the grace has an almost manic superstructure that seems psychiatric. It is accidental and yet also acquired through piety, and with Mechthild it is simply there. Reliable and closely connected to the Minne.

It is a merciless grace, pure awareness. Now it is no longer a model for today, we can no longer muster such tremendous faith fanatic power. Even though we have numerous consciousness researchers, but hardly any awareness researchers, we can only use mysticism as a comparative example. Nevertheless, I attach here an illustration which the psychologist F. Helg has printed after H.

Petzold in his book 'Psychotherapy and Spirituality'.[104] It is an overview composed of eastern mediation and yoga techniques and western Gestalt psychology. I have added to it the terms consciousness (above) and awareness (below) where they fit reasonably well. Admittedly, this picture does not have the precision of far matured science, not even of Lacanian psychoanalysis, where the term 'self' is not used, because it is not logically clarified enough.

Nevertheless, one sees that awareness on the one hand can go up to ecstasy, on the other hand, however, can also be found close to the complete underexcitement (e.g., the intermediate realm in dying) and to the Samadhi, which according to eastern terminology is considered as a

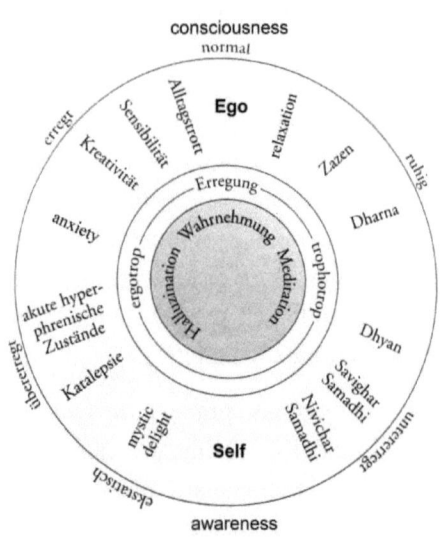

[104] Helg, F., Psychotherapie und Spiritualität (Psychotherapy and Spirituality), Walter (2000) S. 137

state of rest of the mature personality. This scheme re-
minding of the esoteric is basically not to be evaluated
worse than my 'iconic' with 'mountain' or 'sea'. It is true
that one has to go to the academically trained Helg for a
gestalt-therapeutic practice, which Lacan always dis-
missed, because it was already certain what would come
out: the good gestalt, the good form, which is ultimately
determined by the therapist. There is therefore another
possibility of comparison, namely the Kantian 'thing in
itself'.

The Kantian thing in itself was already transformed by
Schopenhauer into the will, i.e. into a process of the subject, because it was simply no longer graspable with a
physical, objective quantity. In Lacan and in *Analytic
Psychocatharsis*, the subject reference is also in the foreground, it revolves around the 'thing', which precisely has
no shape, no preconceived form, but one that counts only
by its sole awareness, and which Lacan always called the
'Ding' in German as a counterpoint to the Other, to l'Autre. It is a striking experience of this 'thing' (Ding), which
for Lacan is precisely not 'la chose', the thing, but rather
some thingness that is empty, hollow like an almost infinite gap, auratic. The psychoanalyst J. Bossinade writes
that the Lacanian 'thing' (Ding) is a kind of extreme sublimation, extreme spiritualization, refinement, so that one
almost has to speak of a maximum self-sublimation,

which can hardly be achieved from a standing start, e.g. without the help of a formula-word.[105]

Thus, to experience the 'thing' (Ding) means to be close to pure awareness, to the highest enjoyment, but also to death. Kant himself only had to look into the sky to be so fascinated by it that he felt looked at. For him the look into the starry sky and the voice of morality in himself was enough to be able to talk about the 'thing in itself'. In my opinion it is about the closest combination of Id Rays (sky heaven outside) / Id Speaks (moral law inside). This correlates in Lacan, on the one hand, around "the Other, whom - if one always meets him in his place - one can also call the 'l'Autre des astres' (the Other of the stars), L'Autre and the 'Ding' because he/it is thus the stable system of the world and of the object."[106] This Lacanian Other and his 'Ding' represent for him together the center of the unconscious and also of the universe.

And because this is now authentically present in each of us, according to Lacan, there is no need for a university teacher, for a master. "The difference between the 'Ding' and the object, the chose," Lacan writes, "is thus, first of all, that the 'Ding' is fundamentally alien, . . in any case,

---

[105] Bossinade, J., Theory of Sublimation: A Key to Psychoanalysis and Kafka's Work, K&N (2007).

[106] Lacan, J., Seminar III, Quadriga (1997) p. 89 where he refers to the constancy of the fixed stars, which like the 'Ding' are always there, although ultimately nothing further can be said of them to the unconscious.

is the first outside as that to which the whole path of the subject is oriented. It is without any doubt a path of control, of reference, in relation to what? - To the world of its desires."[107] I interpret this to mean that we desire too many objects, we are too object-oriented, and so we remain below, too grounded, instead of 'elevating' the object - as Lacan goes on to say - 'to the dignity of the 'Ding,' that is, to sublimate it, to spiritualize it, to refine it in awareness. The 'chose' remaining objects are only capable of consciousness, but not of full awareness.

Quite clearly, the 'Ding' is close to the real and yet different in that it represents rather that which is invisible, the 'void', but which acts precisely because of its apparent nothingness. "The real is without crack, it is a solid, dark, but the 'Ding' is where the other shows itself untranslatable for the subject," writes J. Bossinade.[108] She also writes the following sentence, difficult to understand, though true: "As a result of the appearance of the 'prehistoric Other'[meaning again this kind of earliest father-figure, god, ancestor], the human subject experiences a 'distance' through which it becomes 'alienated' [namely, the "Ding"] from a state that it subsequently imagines as the unbroken real or as a closed womb." A return is thus no longer possible, neither to the psychically so strongly

---

[107] Lacan, J., Seminar VII, Quadriga (1996) S. 66f

[108] Bossinade, J., Theory of Sublimation: A Key to Psychoanalysis and Kafka's Work, K&N (2007).

lingering mother's womb nor to paradise, but the 'Ding' remains with one as emptiness and self-sublimation. It is not nothingness, but it reminds quite strongly again of the awareness as such.

L'Autre is together with the 'Ding' in and around us and gives us the Rays of a star-like being looked at and the Speaks of an orienting sound, which can be brought into a concrete connection in the *Analytic Psychocatharsis*, while in all other descriptions the two always remain separated from each other. It is not nothingness, but it reminds quite strongly again of the awareness as such. Their connection is only invoked (as in Mechthild) or only theorized (as in classical psychoanalysis). The evocation creates a masochistic-manic form, because of which one could have canonized Mechthild anyway. Although always interesting to read, the theorizing of psychoanalysis always lags far behind its own practice.

Therefore the 'Ding' is connected with the awareness of the gap, of the fundamental lack, which is so determining for the human being. Freud already stated that there are three types of discourse to which a relation to the Lacanian 'Ding' correlates exactly. Thus, in art there exists a repression of the 'Ding', in religion there is a displacement, and in the discourse of science it is a matter of the rejection of the 'Ding'. "The discourse of science rejects the presence of the thing, insofar as from its point of view, the ideal of absolute knowledge emerges, that is, the ideal of something that posits the 'Ding' but does not calculate with it. Everyone knows that this view ultimately turns out to be a failure in history. The discourse of science is determined by this rejection, therefore probably - what is rejected by the symbolic, according to my formula, appears in the real - and it amounts to a view in which, at the end of physics, such a mysterious thing as the 'Ding' emerges."[109]

Before I make a comment on physics, briefly a return to Easter Island. No question that in the statues weighing tons there is something of the 'Thing', but also something of the Other, of l'Autre. Quite obviously, the rulers have always placed only one statue next to the other and have also organized a competition for size in order to have as many statues as possible and also to stand there in posterity as a more significant l'Autre. But importance is not created by quantity and rivalry envy. One should have left it at only One and provided it with ever newer and better rock materials. Because the Easter Islanders were great geologists, they could have exported their science all over the world and done their 'thing' ('Ding') that way, if I may say it so boldly.

Nothing can make it clearer that the 'Ding' can only be mediated by such a practice as is offered - for the global space and the present time - in *Analytic Psychocatharsis*, because the 'Ding' is nothing describable, it can only be

---

[109] Lacan, J., Seminar VII, Quadriga (1996) S. 162

experienced individually, in everybody's behalf. In the usual psychotherapeutic (psychoanalytic) consultation, in religion and philosophy, this real cannot be reached, because one does not even get to see the illusory worlds of the 'Ding' such as the 'mountain', the lucidity point or the 'sea', but is only allowed to whisper about its secret behind held hands. One must be allowed to experience the catharsis of the image-acting, of the Rays, of the 'Ding', because as catharsis the 'Ding' has become practice, high-driving, liberating, blissful practice, whose relation to love and death as the 'other way round' I have sufficiently described - also on the basis of Mechthild's great 'visions'.

The 'Ding' is - completely in the Lacanian sense - Mechthild's 'minnecamp, which is not a lottery bed, not a 'chose', but on the contrary, the imaginary-real per se, the unspeakable, the - as quoted - 'first outside' or better 'inside-outside', because it is not localizable. Accordingly, it is not a place at all, but a state, a condition of the subject, if it is realized in awareness. My little 'visions' have the advantage that they do not take me so far away from the everyday and yet they are important and helpful as 'Ding-experience', as entrance into the awareness of the transition to the pass-word, as exit for the 'other way round'.

Of course, the Lacanian 'Ding' is the 'other way round' of his l'Autre, who comes from the word-acting and now in the pass-word may even give the 'Ding' a name, a definite statement. It is necessary to have the high-driving, self-sublimated effect, as Mechthild shows it, but then she cannot give it a modern or even scientific form. The effect of this nothing, brings the emptiness of the 'Ding' in motion, so that it can also make a definite statement as a crowning. No one can chew this out for you, the individual has to achieve this in himself and thus succeed in the fulfilling awareness. The 'thing' as Id Rays/Speaks must be realized as Oneness.

It is clear that this last awareness of the 'Ding' can be experienced preferentially also in the last moments of dying or one will also have knowledge of it in extreme withdrawal in meditation and other body techniques already during life with similar intensity. In the conventional psychoanalyses, as much as I appreciate them and have also practiced them as a therapist, one will never get there, and for the treatment of neuroses it is not even absolutely necessary. But in the case of psychosomatic illnesses and personality or somatization disorders, without a profound switch, it is probably not sufficient to do only conventional therapy.

Tempting to speculation is Lacan's last sentence quoted above about the 'end of physics, where such enigmas as the 'Ding' emerge'. And especially by the now gained knowledge of the full awareness of the 'Ding' on the one hand and of the consciousness, which is still to be found even in matter, as the neuroscientist Tononi stated. Both would fit, nevertheless, to the physical theory of the end, in which one struggles for decades how quantum mechanics and relativity theory could be coordinated. Or also how this coordination is related to psychics, the unconscious and the 'Ding'. But as I said, it remains speculation for now. In the following appendix I discuss the exact practical implementation of the procedure of *Analytic Psychocatharsis*.

Appendix

The procedure of *Analytic Psychocatharsis* is very simple from its practical side - as already described in part. Nevertheless, I will give here a short summary and further *formula-words*.[110] One sits in a comfortable posture and repeat one, two or up to five *formula-words* slowly one after the other purely in the mind, while at the same time one pays attention to whether something appears that has the character of an 'Id *Rays*'. The 'Rays' can be an enlightenment, body image perception, a shimmer, a 'spot of light', or a basic lucidity that is associated with such a phenomenon. So the ray is not something one has to imagine, create or even force oneself. It is present in every human being as the primary form of a drive (sopic-drive) and thus only has to be awakened or expected.

Just as the Id Rays, however, also the mentioned shuddering, 'trickling through' can be felt or the sensation can arise how the own body image shifts, widens or it can simply be determined as a shimmering in front of the closed eyes. Even a dark shimmer is already a perception that can stand out very slightly from the darkness in the head. the sensation can emerge how one's own body im-

---

[110] Further formula words can be found in other publications or on the website given below. For the time being, these are sufficient. You should not need more than five. In this text, more formula-words are given, so that one can start at least with three different ones to perform the two exercises of the procedure.

age shifts,[111] widens or is simply fixed as black paint, as a stain in front of the closed eyes. Because black is already a perception, which can stand out from the darkness in the head quite slightly. No matter what is 'seen' or 'experienced', it will have the character of even a very small 'Id *Rays*', and that is enough.

Thereby a relaxation occurs, a catharsis (purification), a liberation experience, which can be increased particularly by it, if at the same time the said formula words are practiced purely mentally. When, as described in the text, I have sometimes seen the Rays as the 'sea' in my own experiences, I have, however, only paid attention to the Rays that lift one above it and have concentrated more on the wording of the formula words. For they are the ones that steer the first exercise, and precisely in the direction of an indeterminate Rays, i.e. not to any form, not even that of a God as practiced by Mechthild of Magdeburg. It is enough the lucidity, the catharsis, with which one changes to the second exercise, in which every too much image-acting radiance disappears again anyway.

---

[111] This is an experience that has something to do with atavistic emotional reactions. The early humans still felt a lot with their uncovered skin, touched it and communicated in an environment-related way. Even with moving pieces of music, when it grips you like a shiver trickling down your back, we fall back on these particularly deep emotions. In *Analytic Psychocatharsis*, however, this experience is used as confirmation of an insight, e.g. in the *pass-words*.

At the bottom left one can see a different Formula- Word as I have given in the main text. Also this (RA-DIC-IT) is not a normal word from Latin, but it contains several overlapping meanings in one formulation, it is 'linguistically crystalline' like Lacan said from the unconscious. Besides the radiat and dicit (*Rays* and *Speaks*) there are several disparate meanings written in a circle and read from different letters. For example, here one can also use "adi cit r" (approach, it moves R), "C i tradi" (handed over a hundred i), "citra di" (on this side the gods), "dicit ra" (it says ra), "r adic it" (add r, it goes), "radi cit" (get scratched, it moves), "trad ici" (tell, I have met) etc., whereby much sounds quite absurd. But this has no meaning for the formal expression. It is only decisive to be able to clearly explain the scientific reasoning (several meanings in one formulation, use only of other interfaces), and this is very important for the procedure, because this is the only way to have full confidence in the method.

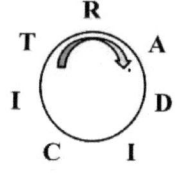

This is the first exercise which is based on actual guidelines of psychoanalysis, because mental reverberation generates a regression (an inner retreat) which at the same time concentrates only on a narrowed aspect of the looking drive, the perceptual instinct (the *Rays*). In addition, *formula-word* repetition takes the place of what in psychoanalysis is called the obligation to repeat, the unconscious repetition. This is at least abolished as long as the exercises of the *Analytic Psychocatharsis* are effective. I have already indicated in the main text that this simplifies and reduces an essential hurdle of classical psychoanalysis. It is important that it comes to a catharsis, to a liberation experience and not only to a simple relaxation. At least for some time one frees oneself from the unconscious obligation to repeat.

As far as other forms of therapy and their problems are concerned, by using *Analytic Psychocatharsis* it is usually possible to avoid them in a simplified way. It is no longer enough simply to believe a therapist or meditation teacher and follow his simple instructions. Nowadays it is also necessary to understand that the method has a scientific basis and that one can and should participate with

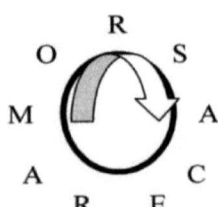

own thoughts. This way, in deeper moments of the exercises dependencies on the ideology of the method, on the teacher or therapist or irrational fears do not occur. The Id *Rays* (crystalline) of the cathartic experience are thus derived from the basic power of the scopic drive. It is therefore something that is originally present in every human being, just like the Id *Speaks* (the linguistic, the uttering).[112]

---

[112] In psychoanalysis we assume that symbolic order or language plays a decisive role in human development, dividing perception into a pure sensory activity and a drive activity. The activity of the senses is a real perception, the activity of

After the R-A-D-I-C-I-T, the *formula-word* O-R-S-A-C-E-R-A-M can be added, because if someone is really interested in learning the analytic pychocathartic method, at least three of these formulations are necessary. Two or even just one would tire one out too quickly. In the *formula-word* C-E-R-A-M-O-R-S-A (picture previous page) - once written differently - there are following meanings depending on initial letter: C eram orsa (I was a hundred times beginning, amo R sacer (I love the holy R), cera morsa (the fragmented wax), mors acer (death is bitter), amor sacer (love is holy), etc.). How to emphasize, one can forget these meanings immediately again. They are too disparate, i.e. cannot be reduced to any denominator. For if one practices them in the uniform lettering, one will never bring together the bitter death with the fragmented wax and the hundredfold beginning in one meaning. It is only important to understand how the *formula-words* are structured, so that one can scientifically-intellectually question the process of any time. If any feelings or ideas arise that are inappropriate or frightening, one can reflect or read more about the process. Blind faith is not required.

In the second exercise, attention is now paid to exactly this *Speaks*, this body echo, i.e. to a sound coming from above / right in the head, to a tone, sound, from the deep inside. After all, these are letters that emanate from this

---

instinct a pleasure of perception, in summary we speak of perceptiveness. The true comes in through language (Id *Speaks*), the perception through reality (Id *Rays*).

'typographic' space and which the unconscious holds stored there. And it is precisely into this space that the *formula-words* have penetrated and have awakened and evoked the letters in their 'B(r)uchstaben'-likeness (broken-letterings). Again, the same applies here: it is a completely original aspect of the drive to express or speak, which is present in every human being as a primary process and even takes on the form of very brief, compact "inner sentences", "ultra-reduced phrases" in the unconscious (all concepts of Lacan for this phonetic experience).

Here, too, at first only a fine noise, a distant sound or similar can be perceived, but the practitioner will notice from the beginning that this is a concentration on a more up-right or up-central hearing system in the head. The echoes of the body have a relationship to this, which is being referred to here. Even if the actual hearing and speech system in the head is left-handed, the more rudimentary, musical and more regression accessible hearing and speech system are present on the right side and its echo structure is clearly recognizable. The short phrases of the *pass-words* are more suitable for this, while the left-sided system (psychoanalytically: the preconscious) plays a role in the longer ones.

In addition again a last example from the experience of one of my adepts of the *Analytic Psychocatharsis*", which I have already published in another book, and which was: "That is not it"! At the first moment it was not quite clear to the practitioner what this meant, but later he came to me with the hunch that it might have to do with the procedure itself. I confirmed this to him, because such an expression is very reminiscent of the typical psychoanalytic 'resistance', that is, the reluctance to have to say everything freely and to reveal too much repressed truth. "This," my method, "is not what it should be," what he had imagined. "This is not it."

This interpretation made sense to him, because now I could explain to him that it was, after all, exactly what *Analytic Psychocatharsis* contains, namely that there can be such a thing at all as a pass-word from one's own inner being, that 'It' actually speaks in one in this way. Moreover, I could refer here to the Other(s), that is, to Lacan's 'L'Autre', which he calls the hoard of signifiers, of units of speech. It is these "important others", of which the psychoanalyst O. Kernberg spoke, which are internalized in one as ego-ideal, super-ego but also as a "deeply empathic understanding ego" and which have unified themselves to the Other. Moreover, the unconscious truth is just not the usual, generally communicated and consciously known truth, but the one with the reversal, the one with the empty space, the 'other way round', which I once called elsewhere the frigid partner in search of the truth, because she is so hesitant (quite different from Mechthild, who is not so squeamish, but does not strive for the truth as such, but takes the more direct, shorter way to certainty, which can also be questionable).

However, the unconscious awakened with modern methods - such as with the Ariadne's thread of R-A-D-I-C-I-T filters out all too questionable and enigmatic statements. In addition, perhaps a little psychoanalytical knowledge is needed to translate such an identity or pass-word into the printable text, which was not too difficult in the case of the saying with "It is not", however, because it was probably about the resisting in the subject himself. Also if someone, as Freud reported with regard to an interpretation to the conflict-related mother-imago, emphasizes with an indignant, affect-laden and loud voice: "No, it is not the mother at all"! it is most likely exactly about the mother. A too vehement defense is in the reversal the confirmation.

If one reads something about psychoanalysis and is keeping in touch with literary, scientific and other cultures, and make an attempt with the exercises, in short: if one is a bit of an educated citizen will interpret the often immediately visible *pass-words* correctly. Thus Freud writes that even some dreams, which are now much more distorted than the *pass-words*, and which come directly from the symbolic-real, could be read directly from the "sheet". It is no longer necessary to ask the dreamer about his ideas and to bring in cumbersome interpretations.

And one last hint, which is often asked for. If one notices during the application of *Analytic Psychocatharsis* that the Id *Rays* portion during practice is too strong, one switches to the Id *Speaks* exercise and vice versa. Otherwise, both exercises should only be performed for about twenty minutes. The change between practical experience and theoretical thinking is important because in the end something in common will emerge: a mental self-awareness, a practical logic, a cathartic analysis. In the end, both exercises find their way to an inner 'mission', to a certainty of 'What's about the ONE',[113] and thus to the possibility of being able to participate in the procedure.

On the other hand, I have already described that sometimes one does not only deviate from the meditative process in thoughts. Sometimes one even deviates between the individual *formula-words* to images, memories, to a mixture of both and to *pass-words*, and yet returns to *formula-word* reversion. The advanced student will experience this as enriching, because he does not allow himself to be seduced into a one-sided direction of radiation or speech, but remains in the progression in the narrow combination of the two basic drives, basic principles, mirroring- and echo-discourse.

Examples of these *pass-words* I have described several in the text. Everybody has to be patient and try out what he thinks is a safe word can. Sometimes it's like you're almost in retrospect, in the final phase of the *pass-word*

---

[113] This concerns the title of my book, also published in English, which deals with the same subject by means of literature and mathematics.

experience, the phrase-hearing the short sentence. Sometimes it seems it's a very, very quiet thought, but still is clear or quite clear. I have to be so vague here, nevertheless there is no doubt about the phenomenon both from the psychoanalytic theory as well as from the many experiences I have had to collect. Even if the actual hearing-talking system in the head is left-sided is laid out, the more rudimentary is on the right side, musical and the regression more accessible auditory Intercom system available.

Again: After the first exercise, the mental repetition of several *formula-words* with a simultaneous occurrence thereof see if you have a ray, a lucidity, a trickle, a liberating, cathartic experience, you move on to the second exercise. Here you concentrate to the sound, the tone, the *Speaks* from above or right inside until you have completely transcended body-consciousness has. If you notice that the ray portion of the training is too much is strong, you switch to the Speech Exercise and vice versa. Each exercise should be performed for about twenty minutes.

The aim of the procedure is to achieve an ideal, successful and satisfying combination of the two exercises. I cannot make any definite specifications here, because when the Ray and *Speaks* exercises, are fulfilling in their combination, everyone should be able to know for himself. After all, the experiences mature in progress with the theory, about which one can read oneself or justify it oneself. The change between practical experience and theoretical thinking is important because in the end something in common will emerge: a mental self-awareness, a practical logic, a cathartic analysis. Ultimately, both exercises can also lead to an inner 'assignment', to a certainty of being able to participate in the shaping of the procedure.

For just as Freud spoke of 'lay analysis' because he did not want to have only academics in his ranks, the argument that the procedure should not depend on professions and titles is even more valid for *Analytic Psychocatharsis*. To this day, analysts worldwide are only physicians and psychologists with university training. Here, the father of psychoanalysis has not been followed, although such a following is required in the essential points. But one can become a scientist also outside the university, which would also help to make the scholastic, university discourse really an analytic discourse.

Bibliography

Baggini, J., Ich denke, also will ich, (I think, so I want) dtv (2016)

Barkhaus, A., Mayer, M., Identität, Leiblichkeit, Normativität (identity, corporeality, normativity (Suhrkamp (1996)

Bauriedl, T., Beziehungsanalyse, (relationship analysis) Suhrkamp (1993)

Benthien, C., Wulf, Ch., Körperteile (body parts), Rowohlt (2001)

Bezzel, C., Wittgenstein, Junius (1996)

Breuer, R., Immer Ärger mit dem Urknall (Always Trouble with the Big Bang), Rowohlt (1993)

Brockman, J., Vogel, S., Wie funktioniert die Welt? (How does the world work), Fischer Taschenbuch (2013)

Byung-Chul Han, Die Austreibung des Anderen (The Expulsion of the Other), Fischer Wissenschaft (201)

Byung-Chul Han, Die Errettung des Schönen (The Salvation of Beauty), Fischer Wissenschaft (201)

Camus, A., Der Mythos des Sisyphos, Rowohlt (2018)

Carnap, R., Einführung in die Philosophie der Naturwissenschaft (Introduction to the Philosophy of Natural Science) (1969)

Damasio, A. R., Descartes` Irrtum, Dtv (1997)

Dennet, D. C., Von den Bakterien zu Bach – und zurück, Suhrkamp (2018)

Davies, P., Gott und die moderne Physik (God and modern physics), Bert. M. (1986)

Eccles, J. C., Gehirn und Seele, Piper (1987)

Eichmeier, J., Höfer, O., Endogene Bildmuster, U&S – Verlag (1974)

Fischer-Lichte, E., Performativität: Eine Einführung, transcript (2012)

Freud, S., Studienausgabe, Fischer (1989)

Goel, B. S. Meditation und Psychoanalyse, Ariston (1989)

Görz, G., Einführung in die Künstliche Intelligenz (Introduction to Artificial Intelligence), Addison-Wesley (1996)

Harari, Y. N., Homo Deus, C. H. Beck (2017)

Heidegger, M., Unterwegs zur Sprache, G. Neske (1959)

Hilbrecht, H., Meditation und Gehirn, Schattauer (2010)

Hofstadter, D., Die Analogie, Klett-Cotta (2014)

Horgan, J., An den Grenzen des Wissens, Luchterhand (1997)

Hustvedt, S., Die gleissende Welt (The blazing Wiorld) Rowohlt (2016)

Husttvedt, S., Das Leiden eines Amerikanmers, Rowohlt (2009)

Hustvedt, S., Wenn Gefühle auf Worte treffen (When feelings meet words) , Kampa (2019)

Jacobs, A., Schrott, R., Gehirn und Gedicht, Hanser (2011

Jakobson, R., Semiotik, Suhrkamp (1988)

Jakobson, R., On Language, Harvard University Press (1995)

Jung. C.G., Gesammelte Werke, Walter (1983)

Kant, I., Kritik der reinen Vernunft, Reclam (1966)

Kluge, F., Etymologisches Wörterbuch, W. de Gruyter (1989)

Lacan, J., Schriften I - III, Walter, (1975)

Lacan, J., Seminare I,I, VII, XI, XX, Quadriga (1980-1995)

Lacan, J., Seminaire Nr. III, Iv, VIII, XVII, Edition Seuil (1981-1994)

Lacan, J., Die Bildungen des Unbewussten, Turia & Kant (2006)

Lacan, J., Mitschriften der Seminare,VI,IX,X,XII,XV, B.R.L.F., Strasbourg

Laplanche, J., Pontalis, J. B., Das Vokabular Der Psychoanalyse, Suhrkamp (1989)

Linke, D., Kunst und Gehirn, Rowohlt (2001)

Maar, C., Pöppel, E., Christaller, T., Die Technik auf dem Weg zur Seele, Rowohlt (1996)

Merleau-Ponty, M., Das Sichtbare und das Unsichtbare (The Visible and the Invisible) Fink Verlag (1994)

Pinker, S., Der Sprachinstinkt, Kindler (1996)

Plato, Sämtliche Werke, Insel Verlag (1991)

Popper, K. R., Eccles, J. C., Das Ich und sein Gehirn, Piper (1989)

Potthoff, P., Die Begegnung der Subjekte (The Encounter of Subjects), Psychosozial-Verlag (2014)

Roazen, D., Der innere Sinn, Archäologie eines Gefühls (The Inner Touch, Archaeology of Feeling), Fischer (2012)

Roheim, G., Die Panik der Götter (The Panic of the Gods), Kindler (1975)

Rosset, C., Das Reale in seiner Einzigartigkeit (The real in its uniqueness), Merve (2000)

Rüdinger, D., Perrez, M., Anthropologische Aspekte der Psychologie, O. Müller (1979)

Rudgley, R., Abenteuer Steinzeit (Adventure Stoneage), Kremaye & Scheriau (2001)

Schmidt-Hellerau, C., Lebenstrieb & Todestrieb (Life Drive & Death Drive), Libido & Lethe, Verlag Intern. Psychoanalyse (1995)

Searle, J. R., Geist, Hirn und Wissenschaft, Suhrkamp (1992)

Seidler, G. H., Der Blick des Anderen (The View of the Other), Verlag Intern, Psychoanalyse (1995)

Sinz, R., Gehirn und Gedächtnis, Fischer Utb (1981)

Strowik, E., Sprechende Körper (Speaking Bodies), Fink-Verlag (2009)

Thompson, R. F., Das Gehirn, Spectrum (1994)

Thorne, K. S., Gekrümmter Raum und Verbogene Zeit, Knaur (1996)

Tipler, F. J., Über die Omegapunkttheorie, Piper (1994)

Uexküll, Th., Fuchs, M., Subjektive Anatomie, Schattauer (1994)

Weiss, Der Andere in der Übertragung (The Other in Transference), Frommann-Holzboog, (1988)

Weizsäcker, C. F. von, Die Einheit der Natur (The Unity of Nature), Dtv (1995)

Weinberg, S., Der Traum von der Einheit des Universums, Bertelsmann (1993)

Weizenbaum, J., Die Macht der Computer, Stw (1977)

Wiener, O., Probleme der Künstlichen Intelligenz, Merve (1990)

Wilhelm, R., Informatik, C.H.Beck (1996)

Wilson, E. O., Der Wert der Vielfalt, Piper (199

Wolf, F. A., Die Physik der Träume, Byblos (1996)

Wygotski, L. S., Denken und 'Sprechen (Thinking and 'Speaking)', Fischer (1981)

Books published in English by the author

The physically sick Soul

In this booklet of only forty pages, the author describes in a simplified form the method of *Analytic Psychocatharsis* that he developed. It is not only about the mentally ill soul, but also about the treatment of the disorder expressed in a more physical form.

What about the ONE

The One is only insufficiently described in mathematics. It is about the spiritual-physical unity of man, which can only be achieved through a combination of psychoanalytical and meditative exercises. The author describes this process using the literature of Siri Hustvedt and other female authors as well as the psychoanalysis of J. Lacan.

A Path to self-analytical Practice

The vertical Ego

Our usual social Ego is oriented horizontally, but the essential and still predominantly unconscious Ego is oriented in the vertical. This is connected with primary inner psychic reflections, which are not exactly captured by psychoanalysis, because it is more oriented to the word. With a few meditative exercises one can reach the sufficiently good vertical and unite it with the

Life while Dying, a treatise on Sisyphus and on a new Self-practice for today

Outsmarting Death two Times.

Sisyphus managed to outsmart death twice before he finally had to roll the big stone up the hill in Hades. Today's man has it better, for whom in the meantime it is proven that after his medically determined death still brain activities are perceptible. By the procedure of the analytic psychocatharsis he can use them to postpone the death by an important experience.

Further books by the author from MCS-Verlag in German

Analytic Psychocatharsis

Psychoanalytic theory and cathartic meditation cannot simply be transferred into each other. If, however, both methods are related by a decisive element (formula words containing several meanings in one stroke), a new method of one's own can be established. Psychoanalysis and meditative methods are discussed, and the practice of one's own procedure is described in detail.

The Revolt of the Self

The classical method of analysis of the unconscious represents a too theoretical revolt of the self. In order to be successful in practice, a more direct self-analytic procedure is required, which everyone can develop out of themselves. Formulations that contain several meanings in a single stroke of writing can break up the unconscious of each individual through mental practice and free him or herself.

'teadrunken' The starting point of the book is the doctrine of the psychoanalyst O. Earl Wittgenstein, who assumed that man contains three parts within himself, which he can only combine in different ways to form a unity or uniform personality. He calls the ultimate and ideal unity the 'trialogue'. On the basis of the description of several mountain climbs, the author roams through all possible cultural and psychological questions in order to achieve the 'trialogue' through hiking, meditation and intellectual processing. The book will be published in English end of 2021

Yoga and Psychoanalysis

Based on a scientific biography of the religious scientist and yoga teacher Kirpal Singh (Surat Shand Yoga), all forms of yoga are compared from the perspective of psychoanalysis. It is necessary to establish a procedure of one's own, which the author also calls *Analytic Psychocatharsis*. Numerous pictures and diagrams make the book attractive.